FOLK GUITAR AS A PROFESSION

BY HAPPY TRAUM

Guitar Player Books
(An affiliate of Guitar Player Magazine)
Learning Materials For The Complete Guitarist

JOHN SEBASTIAN

FOREWORD

Happy Traum and I grew up in the same town. Lucky for us it happened to be New York City. Our interest in folk music coincided perfectly with a national movement, one focus of which was Washington Square Park. As never before in history, regional musics of all types collided and combined in that cement circle at the foot of 5th Avenue. Of course each of us, when quizzed about our future, would mutter something about it all being a hobby and how our actual source of livelihood would come from somewhere else. And now it's fifteen years later and each of us is still drawing in some way from that fertile ground.

Folk Guitar As A Profession is more than instruction for the budding accompanist. Besides providing access to style after style of guitar playing, Happy suggests different ways of tackling the music business itself, showing you the contracts, riders, and publishing deals. He tells you when to get a lawyer, when you may have to do without a manager, and what exactly those booking agents do. He interviews a publisher about audition tapes and a famous friend about the life of a studio musician. His suggestions of where to play and how to equip yourself leave plenty of room for your own aspirations.

Wherever you're planning to put your effort and inspiration, this book can provide some real help. And it's coming from a friend.

John Sebastian
Woodstock, NY

CREDITS

Photography
Ashley Famous Agency: page 41
John Blakemore: page 21
Michael Brooks: page 49
Capitol Records: page 15
Jim Crockett: pages 28, 55
Len DeLessio: page32
Fantasy: pages 12, 31
David Gahr: page 57
Guild Guitars: page 6
Guitar Player Magazine: page 50
Bob Krueger: page 40
Veryl Oakland: page 13
Ceci Sebastian: cover, foreword
Takoma Productions: page 9
Pascal Valentin: page 50
Dick Whiteford's Promotional and
    Personal Management Agency: page 22

Library of Congress Catalog Card Number: 76-57470

International Standard Book Number: 0-89122-015-1

Design/Layout
Sandy Haight

Photocomposition
Frank Fletcher

Administrative Assistant
Marcia Hartman

Editor
Dominic Milano

Executive Editor
Jerry Martin

Special thanks to Jim Crockett, publisher of
Guitar Player Magazine, for his helpful guidance.

For information on distribution to the
music trade and the book trade contact
Guitar Player Books, Box 615, Saratoga, CA 95070.

CONTENTS

INTRODUCTION

As I sit down to write this book, several difficulties face me that I should get out of the way right from the beginning. The first and most immediate is the inherent contradiction between the words "folk" and "profession" in the title.

When I started playing the guitar back in 1954, the idea that I would ever make money from my music was the farthest thing from my mind. I played for the love of the music and making something myself, the way people love to carve wood or tinker with engines. I played folk music because I was fascinated and excited by the story that each folk song seemed to tell, and the weight and drama of history that seemed to hang from each note. The guitar became the vehicle which helped bring these stories to life. The spirit inherent in the earliest years of my playing is still the embodiment of my concept of folk music, and so it seems slightly strange now that I am writing this book from the viewpoint of a "professional."

Actually, in those early days of the folk revival in New York City, there were very few singers or guitarists who could be called professional. The folk music enthusiasts who hung out in Washington Square and traded songs and licks were a small and dedicated (sometimes downright fanatical) group of individuals pursuing various paths towards the understanding and playing of traditional music. Most of these people were young, and those who weren't students had regular "day jobs".

Later, as the folksong movement started to catch on, many of these people whom I had known as enthusiastic but somewhat scruffy amateurs had become guitar teachers, songwriters, accompanists, studio musicians, instrument makers, folklorists, recording engineers, and even internationally-famous stars. *Professionals*. And although some sold out to the blandly inane, washed-out popularizations of folk music typified by the televised *Hootenanny* show, others dug deep into the powerful well-springs of ethnic traditional style, creating an amalgam of the old and the new that changed the form and content of American popular music and song.

So, one of my difficulties is in trying to balance the philosophical differences between my concept of folk music as being an intimate, communal, homemade form of expression, and trying to tell someone how to go about "making it" in the commercial music marketplace, using folk music as the medium for success. Throughout this book I'll throw in some of my aesthetic preferences and hope that you, the reader, will follow your own instincts, judgment, and good taste in pursuing your career as a "folk" musician.

Another thing we'll have to get out of the way is to come to some definition of what we mean by folk guitar and folk music. When we speak of "professional" folk guitar playing, it usually conjures up images of facile performers entertaining large audiences in concert, on TV, or on records. Many of the greatest guitarists do not fall anywhere near this image. Where, in the spectrum of professional guitar playing do you place Rev. Gary Davis, Skip James, Joseph Spence, and Mississippi John Hurt? These musicians, among many others, have directly influenced more than a few city-bred guitarists of other generations and outlooks who have also made significant contributions to continuing traditional guitar styles. The difference between these generations is not in their professionalism—both have their own high standards and values—but in their relationship to their communities. Traditional folk music originated with the need of a particular person (or group) to express themselves musically, and they did so with the support of, and dependency on, their community and its musical standards. It has only been during the past half-century that folk music has left the intimate confines of the ethnic community from which it sprang to become known and loved (for whatever reasons) in the infinitely wider community of mass popular culture.

Most of us who play what is called folk guitar are drawing from a multitude of musical sources and play an amalgam of styles—Delta blues, cowboy songs, Carolina fingerpicking, western swing, Elizabethan lute music, and so on—and to the majority of listeners a folk guitarist is anyone who plays an acoustic guitar and sings. This is all right, unless it prevents the audience from examining what it is about traditional music that makes it special and often great. Most important, it should not prevent you, the folk guitarist, from exploring it and understanding it as well.

Very few professional folk guitarists can separate their guitar work from other things they do, especially their singing. Most folk guitarists use the guitar, however skillfully, as a vehicle for putting across stories or ideas in song. True, there are some notable exceptions, such as John Fahey, Bert Jansch, or Leo Kottke, who are known primarily as instrumentalists, but most folk musicians I know cannot be classified as only "folk guitarists." They are much more than that. In fact, some of my favorite guitarists play very simply, and use the guitar *only* as an accompanying instrument. Jack Elliott and Ritchie Havens are two examples that come immediately to mind. Their playing is rhythmic and stylistically distinctive, if not known for its technical expertise, and they would be the last to call themselves "professional folk guitarists." Still, what they convey through their instrument is essential to their art, and there is a lesson to be learned for every would-be professional.

The field of folk guitar is so wide, so diverse, that it is difficult to know which musical areas to confine ourselves to within the scope of this book. We speak of blues, ragtime, bluegrass, old-time mountain, or country flatpicking, and it all fits nicely into the general mold of "folk guitar." But as expertise grows and musical style changes with it, becoming more sophisticated, the lines begin to blur. When does bluegrass flatpicking become Nashville pop? When does fancy blues playing become jazz? Because someone plays an acoustic guitar are they automatically a folk guitarist, but when they electrify it they become something else?

These are questions that can (and have) been debated for years, so now that I've started things off, I'll get on to the information that I assume you bought this book to find out. Since I don't know you, I can only guess that you're someone who plays but would like to become a performer and get paid for it. Do you sing, want to be an accompanist, part of a band, a lead guitarist on sessions? I don't know. I'll try to give you as many leads as I know, or can find out from others. I'll assume that you already play to a certain extent, and are interested in, and involved with, some aspect of traditional folk music. There are so many directions you can go, even within the confines of this field, that it will be impossible to answer everyone's questions about everything. I'll use as a guide the questions that are most frequently asked of me by people who write or meet me in my travels.

I sincerely hope that this will be more than just a book on how to use your talents for financial gain. I'd like to give you a sense of the roots, style, and underlying philosophy that once drew me to folk music, and has held me ever since. I'll try to introduce you to some new people, songs, and styles if I can. Without a deep commitment to the music and its values, your professionalism won't be worth anything more than money, and that is a hollow goal for any artist.

GETTING STARTED

BREWER AND SHIPLEY

As a folk guitarist, there are several routes that can be taken towards becoming a professional, and a variety of ways that you can apply your trade once you've gotten there. As I see it, though, there are two main roads that you can take, each one a different kind of commitment for you, the artist, and your audiences. One is the commercial pop/folk market, which is where the big money is—the higher-class clubs, large concert halls, major record labels, publicity, TV, the works. Obviously, this is the most difficult end of things to break into, and entails the highest cost in many ways. The other route is the underground, grassroots level that is special to the folk field. Although you can never become rich financially, one can do very well in this milieu, especially with the steady, hard work that it takes to build up a dedicated following. You can also be your own boss by not having to pay all those dues to agents, managers, executives, etc.

I don't mean to lay any value judgments on either of these ways, although I'm sure my own inclinations will show through. Both routes can be legitimate and done with dignity and responsibility to oneself and the music one represents. I'll try to explore both of these routes in more detail, giving you an idea of what each entails and where it can take you. Since they are not quite so cut and dried as I have laid them out, they will overlap a great deal, as you will see.

Let's start at the beginning. I'll assume that you are a guitarist who plays pretty well and also sings. You have explored many of the dominant folk styles, but have not gotten them down to an individual style of your own yet. Perhaps you write some songs of your own, but you also have a pretty good repertoire of other people's songs. Hopefully, you have a fairly good background in traditional folk music and guitar styles as well, since this is the foundation on which your music will stand. There is one problem: despite the fact that you feel that you have talent and material, you rarely get to perform, and when you do, it's not for money. Before we go any further I should say tht you are not alone, and that even musicians of long standing and proven ability often find it hard to get work. Please keep in mind that, in the light of this, I can't give you any guaranteed formulas for success. I can only offer some hints as to which direction to go and some traps to avoid.

If you live in a small town or a rural area you will find yourself at an immediate disadvantage (ironic for a folk singer) in that most of the activity is happening in the urban centers. Some small cities around the country may have folk clubs and occasional gatherings of like-minded people who enjoy picking together as a hobby. This is fine for learning, expanding your repertoire, and getting some experience playing in front of an audience, but most people who want to make a living musically wind up at some point in their lives in a big city—

New York, Los Angeles, San Francisco, Atlanta, Nashville, Seattle, etc. If you live far from one of these centers the idea of trying to break into a city scene can be a frightening prospect, but unfortunately it is almost impossible to make a name as a performer without going to a city.

This does not mean that you can't get your basic stuff together in other places. There are small clubs, coffee houses, college campuses, and even roadhouse bars where you can gain valuable experience in stage presence, poise, and audience communication—enormously important to a performer, sometimes as important to your success as your music.

The places you choose to play can be important too, as you'll immediately find out from personal experience. If you are a quiet solo singer or guitarist you'll learn to stay away from bars, which are often pretty rowdy, and play for "listening" audiences at coffee houses or folklore groups. As a guitarist in a country music band, though, you'll do great in the roadhouse circuit, especially if you include some Hank Williams songs in your act. Of course, there is a challenge in taking on any job you can get, and the experience and satisfaction gained in winning over a tough crowd can be worth the trouble.

Perhaps at this point I should tell you a little more about how I got into playing. Although this is just one man's experience, I think it will serve as a pretty fair example of what lots of other musicians go through as well.

Very often there is a fine line between being an amateur and a professional. I can't remember exactly when I first got paid to play, but I know I didn't just go out and say, "Now I'm going to get a job as a professional musician." I started playing at parties for friends, then getting invited to parties because I could play (payment enough at that time). In my freshman year at college I played at a drunken fraternity party and they passed the hat (not before many of them had passed out) and I made about $12 for six hours of playing plus all the beer I could guzzle. I gained some valuable experience in those days (though no money) touring hospitals, old age homes, and schools for the retarded with a group of folk singers.

While I was in college I started getting guitar students, and found that I could help support myself by teaching. I also taught guitar and folk groups at summer camps, and in the fall I would hire a hall in Manhattan and give my own concerts/ songfests to an audience of ex-campers, guitar students, family and friends. I usually came out a little ahead financially, and we all had a good time.

Meanwhile I continued picking at parties, hanging out in The Folklore Center, in Greenwich Village, and playing at unpaid "hoots" at folk clubs. I even made the obligatory hitchhiking trip to the Southern Mountains to meet the "real folk." Eventually I began to get small jobs—some so small they barely existed. I accompanied a strange variety of singers, playing in run-down clubs in New York one night and the Waldorf Astoria another. One singer whom I was backing up ran off with both our fees in his pocket leaving me stranded and broke somewhere in Connecticut. I've not seen him since, except in the movies—he went to Hollywood where he usually plays a bad guy—typecast, no doubt.

On my first trip to the West Coast I started picking informally in a bar in Sausalito, California. The owner liked the music and invited me to stick around and play for free drinks. Well, that was *some* kind of payment. As the evening wore on I had had enough to drink when a customer at the bar offered to buy me one. Not wanting him to spend his money unnecessarily, I naively refused, at which point the owner became furious with me and threw me and my guitar out. In the space of about

an hour I had been hired and fired from a job I never really had to start with.

Why am I telling you all this? Because this is supposed to tell you "where to start" and there is no such place. No one has the answer to that, including the people I know who have "made it" in the music business. They have all scrounged around, played in dives, passed the basket, got burned, took lessons, gave lessons, played with bands, without bands, and stuck to it through the good scenes and the bad scenes until something happened that allowed them to be called "professional." The best of them maintained their love and respect of music without being tainted and corrupted by the smell of money and success. Not that money *necessarily* corrupts (an empty stomach is even more corrupting), but money, fame, and power can become ends in themselves, making the performer sell out the value and beauty of the joy of making music. Without that indefinable spirit, the music loses everything it was intended to do, and becomes little more than a fancy variety of noise.

What I would like to do in the pages that follow is outline a guide to help you enter into that realm of "professionalism" with the least amount of pain, bad moves, and frustrations that will stand in the way of the good music. Most of my advice is based, necessarily, on my own experiences, plus those of some people who have had more experience than I have in certain areas. I hope I can answer your particular questions, but many things cannot, by definition, be answered in a book. They must be learned by trial and error, experience and hard knocks, by you alone. Your path will be yours and no one else's, as will be your music.

LEARNING THE GUITAR

JOHN FAHEY

I assume that if you are thinking of becoming a professional folk guitarist you already play some folk guitar. I think, however, that it would be a good idea at this point to lay down some guidelines for the study of traditional guitar styles for those who are not as skillful as they feel they should be, so that when the time comes to do something in a professional way, you'll really have it together.

The main difference between folk guitar and other kinds of playing is the *style* of the music, but technique is important no matter what you play. It is good, therefore, to expand your musical studies and corresponding guitar playing to cover many different areas. Solid technique is important whether you are playing bluegrass, blues, ragtime, contemporary song accompaniments, or any of the other styles that come under the folk category. (Once again, I should mention that one can be a successful folk singer or entertainer without necessarily being a great guitarist. Many people have done very well with only a limited knowledge of the guitar, relying on vocal style, showmanship, or fine backup musicians to fill in the musical gaps.)

Traditionally, folk musicians learned from other musicians in their family or community, or from itinerant travelers passing through. A typical example of the traditional learning method was told to me by Brownie McGhee. After his father gave him "one of those little old stripey-back toy ukuleles that would never stay in tune," he started picking things out on piano and guitar on his own. Later, he met someone who changed his whole outlook on playing. In his words, "This feller came out of North Carolina in one of my last years in high school. I never will forget him...called him T.T. Carter. He was a very good blues player. I had a little shack then, so all the traveling musicians and guitar players, well, everyone would send them to me. I was very impressed with this guy even though T.T. Carter was never known, and after he left I just fell in love with the guitar all of a sudden. The people in my early life that had the most influence on my music were unknown musicians who never did any recording, or if they did it didn't get around much. There was a feller named Steve Totter and I called him the Master Musician. Him and my father played together, but he played all stringed instruments. That three-stringed thing that we called the zither then (dulcimer); and he also played mandolin, ukulele, violin, bass, guitar and piano.... I used to sit and watch him.... My father was a very good guitarist. Not professionally known, but after a hard day's work he relaxed his mind. From that I got my musical education." [From *Guitar Styles Of Brownie McGhee*, by Brownie McGhee and Happy Traum, Oak Publications, New York.]

Some people are still fortunate enough to have parents from whom they can learn traditional music, but there are few communities nowadays where great itinerant musicians pass through for the price of a meal or a place to stay. Still, it's possible to learn in the traditional way if you make the right contacts or are lucky enough to be in the right place at the right time. Stefan Grossman, Larry Johnson, Roy Bookbinder, and others learned directly from Rev. Gary Davis. They studied with him and acted, on occasion, as his "lead boys," helping him get around in the traditional way that younger men led blind musicians (Leadbelly and Josh White were both lead boys for Blind Lemon Jefferson). I spent a lot of time with Brownie McGhee, learning guitar and many other things from him. I know others who have been able to study with Doc Watson, Jesse Fuller, Mance Lipscomb, and Joseph Spence. Mike and Peggy Seeger grew up in the same house with Elizabeth Cotten and learned some of her guitar style almost by osmosis. But for most people, a perfectly acceptable way to learn is by taking lessons from a music teacher—as long as he can teach you the styles you want to learn.

My first teacher was a disaster, a middle-aged hack who bored me to tears. I told him I wanted to learn to play folk guitar, so he produced from his briefcase an utterly boring method book and had me playing "Home On The Range," picking out the notes on the first two strings. I wanted to accompany myself with Dust Bowl ballads and blues, work songs, and topical songs of social significance. Unfortunately he didn't know Woody Guthrie from Woody Woodpecker. After a short, frustrating time I found another teacher who started me off on the things I wanted to know, and I happily took it from there.

In most areas of the country now there are guitar teachers who have learned to play and teach traditional folk styles, but you have to search them out. If possible, try to find a teacher who has a real love for traditional music and wants to impart his enthusiasm to others. Of course, if you want to start but can't find such a teacher or friends who will help you along, you will still learn a lot about music and the guitar from a jazz or rock teacher, and you'll certainly be able to transfer your technique to any style you choose to play.

If you live in a city, there may be a music school nearby that specializes in guitar, and hopefully folk guitar as well. I know of a few: *The Guitar Study Center* and *Fretted Instruments* in New York City; *The Guitar Workshop* in Roslyn, Long Island; *The Old Town School of Folk Music* in Chicago; *McCabe's* in Los Angeles; and *The Denver Folklore Center* in Denver, Colorado. I assume that private teachers are practically everywhere, but you'll have to scout them out pretty carefully. Many people who claim to be "folk guitar" teachers don't know much more than "Red River Valley," three chords and two strums. You may have to travel some to find a really good player and teacher.

Among the other ways to learn to play, by far the most popular is through the use of an instruction book. Ten years ago there was little available beyond the most simple strums and song accompaniments, but today there are excellent books on every aspect of folk guitar picking. Although the market is flooded with hundreds of folk guitar methods, both good and bad, the best of them are easy to work with and very informative, with some of the most knowledgeable and dedicated writer/musicians as authors. Most of these books use both music and tab (tablature), and some recent instruction books have a small bound-in record so that you can hear the sounds you are striving to get. Since folk music is primarily an aural art, many of the sounds are almost impossible to write down, so the record is an incredibly helpful tool for the learning musician.

Oak Publications (33 W. 60th St., New York, NY 10023), the first company to produce top-quality instruction books on all aspects of folk music and lore, is starting to include a bound-in sound sheet (record) in every folk music instruction book they produce. There are many other companies offering record/book instruction combinations (just look through the pages of *Guitar Player Magazine*), and recently Stefan Grossman, an excellent folk and blues guitarist,

started his own record company, Kicking Mule Records, devoted to teaching folk and blues styles.

In experimenting with forms of instruction, I have come up with one that I think is the next-best thing to a 'live' teacher. Some years ago I started Homespun Tapes, on which some other performers and I teach folk and rock styles on tapes and cassettes in an informal, easy-going way that is as close as I could get to actually giving guitar lessons in person. If you are interested in this kind of instruction, you can write me c/o Homespun Tapes, Box 694, Woodstock, NY 12498, and I'll be glad to send you information on these lessons.

Still another way of learning songs, styles, and techniques, is to pick with other players, especially those who are better than you. Folk festivals, parties, clubs, etc. are all good places for getting together with some other pickers to trade licks, ask questions, and get to know how others are learning their trade. Use a portable tape or cassette recorder if you have one. Most folk or bluegrass festivals have instrumental workshops and you might have an unforgettable session with someone like Doc Watson, Dave Bromberg, Dan Crary, or other professional or traditional folk artists [see the section on concerts and festivals].

Once again, I must emphasize that in folk guitar, style is at least as important as technique, for without it you'll be playing notes out of context, without meaning. Take every opportunity that you can to hear real traditional musicians (not just interpreters), at concerts and festivals, on tapes or records, or even on film. (There have been a few excellent short films made during the past few years documenting traditional musicians and their lives.) Steep yourself in the language and culture of traditional music. It doesn't matter whether it is of the Southern Mountains, Mississippi Delta, or the Scottish Highlands. Learn as much as you can about the people and the music they make, why they make it, how they feel about it. This kind of background work will supply you with a knowledge of all the various styles of playing, and will enhance the depth of your own music.

By this time you might be asking, "If I want to be a pro, make money, get famous, why do I have to go through all this purist crap? There are plenty of guitarists who are making it, and they sound good too, without worrying about how traditional they are. Can't I just learn the guitar and do my thing?"

To be truthful, I suppose you can. I doubt that most of the people out there making a living as folk guitarists really know the field they claim to be representing. What I'm talking about is the ideal, the hope that if the study of traditional music and other forms becomes a part of your music, we will all benefit from it. The best in the field know whereof they speak (or play), and their music enhances the quality of our lives.

REVEREND GARY DAVIS

REPERTOIRE

GORDON LIGHTFOOT

Okay, so you can play the guitar. Now what music do you play?

There are many possibilities, many of them stemming from the previous discussion. My advice is, no matter what you are going to play, learn as many different styles as you can. The more you know, the easier it will be to write, accompany, or perform your own songs in your own style. We are fortunate to have at our disposal an incredible wealth of good material that can be as contemporary today as when it was first sung or played. Traditional music can also become the basis for new material that you or someone else might write or arrange for guitar.

Be selective in choosing the songs you are going to perform. Like every other field, some folk songs are great, others are valuable only in a historical perspective and not as performance pieces. The main thing is to take a song and tailor it to your own particular style of playing. As you gain experience, you will find that your material takes on a flavor and ambience that is yours alone. It is a mysterious thing, but it happens sooner or later, almost without your realizing it. That is when you move from being imitative of other musicians to having your own musical personality. In choosing your material then, you can find those songs that suit what you want to say musically.

Each individual finds something that he likes about certain songs, so I can't tell you what to play. You may lean more heavily towards funky old-time music, or you may perform your own contemporary songs exclusively. In my case bout 50% of my reper-toire is traditional American folk music; 25% consists of my own original songs; and the remaining 25% is made up of contemporary songs written by others. I learn most of my songs from records, but some I get from books and others from friends and singers. The ones I write myself present little problem once I've written them, but the tunes I took from books took time to figure out until I learned to read notes.

Although few traditional folk musicians read music, I think it's a great help to have a working knowledge of music for the guitar. Many great songs that you might be able to get from books would be out of reach if you couldn't read music. And learning to read music is one of the best ways I can think of to increase your repertoire.

EQUIPMENT

LEO KOTTKE

GUITARS

Your first and foremost necessity in terms of equipment is a good-sounding acoustic guitar. Most folk guitarists prefer steel (bronze-wound) strings over the classical-type nylon strings, but there is no hard and fast rule. If you want to vary your sound, you may want to use several different guitars during the course of a program; e.g. steel strings for bluesy or hard-driving songs, classical guitar for quiet ballads, and perhaps a 12-string for heavily rhythmic, full-bodied sounds. Although one guitar will produce a number of different sounds, some guitarists prefer the variety and subtlety that different guitars lend to a show.

The guitar has been the backbone of American traditional music for over a century, and even with the ascendance of the electric guitar and folk-rock sounds, the flat-top, round-hole, 14-fret acoustic is still the favorite of folk, blues, and bluegrass musicians.

Traditional musicians tend to like traditional guitars, and Martin and Gibson are the two favorites in the U.S., Canada, and Europe. For most musicians, the older the guitar the better, and a prize among guitarists is a pre-War (World War II) Martin or Gibson. Good guitars improve with age, and the older guitars have a rich, full sound that the newer ones don't yet have. Many feel that these instruments were also more finely crafted (like everything else), and some of those old instruments just *feel* good. You don't have to go back thirty or forty years to find a good guitar, though. My current Martin D-18 is a 1960 model, and it has a beautiful sound.

I asked Doris Abrahams, of Matt Umanov's Guitar Shop in Greenwich Village, (specializing in old acoustic folk guitars) about her experience with pre-War models. She replied: Pre-War instruments *are* prized among guitarists. However, they are constructed much more lightly than newer models and tend to develop more problems (loose braces, cracks, swelling under the bridge, etc.) when subjected to heavy use. (Airplane handling is deadly.) Post-War guitars, are more heavily constructed and can stand up to a lot more abuse—something to be considered if one is looking for a "road" guitar.

There are many other excellent guitars on the market today, and the one you choose will depend on your taste and your pocketbook. I'd suggest that if you are in the market for a new guitar you go to a shop where there are many choices, sit down for a couple of hours, and play them all until you find the one you like best. Each guitar is different, even guitars of the same model turned out in the same day by the same factory, so you'll have to find the one with the action, tone, neck, and feel that suits you.

Another way to go is to have a guitar custom-built for you. There are several excellent craftsmen around the country who hand-make custom guitars. A guitar manufactured completely by hand in a small-scale operation is bound to cost more, but you'll get exactly what you want, since you'll probably have some personal dealings with the luthier (guitar maker). Unfortunately, custom builders seem to set up and go out of business on a weekly basis. I could give you some names of people I've heard of, but they may no longer be in business by the time this book is published.

If you are down on your money and don't want or need the prestige of a high-class axe, there are several imported imitations of U.S. models, and some of them are quite good. There is one very important factor that should be considered when choosing a lower-priced guitar, though. Is the top made of solid spruce or plywood?

There are literally hundreds of brands (both domestic and imported) that use plywood for their tops. This is undesirable (especially in steel-string models). Here's why: The top is the soundboard of the instrument. Sound is produced by striking the strings, which vibrate and cause the top to vibrate in certain patterns. The vibration of the top causes the air inside the box to vibrate. If the top is made of three layers of wood (plywood) with the grain of each layer going in opposing directions, it will not vibrate freely and will give less sound. Manufacturers use plywood because it is strong, and it lets them cut costs by using less bracing underneath. If it is not braced carefully, the enormous tension exerted by the strings can cause the top to pull up in the bridge area, thus raising the action, which consequently makes the guitar unplayable (and unrepairable). Poor bracing can also cause the top to cave-in at other stress points.

There are a number of moderately-priced guitars on the market that are made with solid spruce tops and are built fairly carefully. Most are Japanese, and are built by very large companies that manufacture the same guitars under different names. Some of the current good ones are: Takamine, Tama, Alvarez-Yairi, and Angelica. These brands have mostly plywood-top guitars, but put out a limited number of solid spruce models. An experienced eye can determine the nature of the top by looking along the edge of the soundhole to see if the wood is layered (plywood) or if it has a consistent grain all the way through (solid wood). You can also read the literature on the different models put out by the manufacturer and choose only those that have a solid spruce top.

One more thing. A good solid, hardshell case is absolutely essential to the life of a guitar that travels. Avoid gig bags, or any lightweight (cardboard; fiberboard) cases—they are death to an acoustic guitar. The extra expense of a good case is well worth it.

STRINGS

As with guitars, strings come in a wide variety of brands and configurations, and a real string freak will know every gauge number, alloy, and number of windings on any given string. For those of us who aren't quite so technically minded, there are four basic string gauges, or thicknesses: heavy, medium, light, and extra-light. These gauges will vary slightly from one brand of strings to the other, and it will take some experimenting to find the one you like best.

Heavy-gauge strings are a favorite with bluegrass guitarists (who also tend to like high-action guitars) who use the instrument primarily for rhythmic backup with plenty of bass runs. The heavier the gauge, the more volume and depth you get, especially in the bass. Also, you can play a heavier-gauge string a lot harder without encountering too much buzzing or string breakage.

One note of warning, however. According to Doris Abrahams: "Heavy-gauge strings are not recommended for any brand of flat-top guitar. They exert an enormous amount of tension that can damage your instrument, particularly if you have an older or cheaper lightweight instrument. Stick with light- or medium-gauge strings."

Light- and *medium-gauge* strings are better all-around strings for both accompaniment and solo work. The type you choose will depend primarily on your particular

touch, the sound you like, and the action of your guitar (the light-gauge strings are easier to fret). Some people mix lights and mediums, using the heavier strings in the bass, and the lights in the treble, or vice versa. Take the time to try different combinations.

Extra-light-gauge strings have the thinnest sound, and are favored by lead players who like to bend strings a lot, and by those who have a very light touch and want to play fast. They are also very good if you are using a pickup, or have a sound system that is so good that the quiet sound of the guitar is not a limitation.

The main disadvantage of using light-gauge strings is that if your guitar is not set up for them, or if your touch is too heavy, you will get a lot of string buzz and fret noise.

There are dozens of brands of strings on the market, and since I haven't tried them all I'd be hard-pressed to give an absolute recommendation of one over all the others. I can tell you, though, that I have been using D'Merle, D'Angelico, and Darco strings for several years with good results. Recently, though, I have switched to a custom brand of my own called Homespun Strings, which I like better than any I have tried before. I now use light-gauge bronze-wound steel strings on my Martin D-18, although I have also used medium-gauge strings as well.

Other brands of high-quality strings that have been recommended by my friends include: D'Addario, Martin, GHS, and Ernie Ball. You have to find the brand and gauge that responds best to your guitar and touch.

Here are some of the standard string sizes (There will be some variation from brand to brand.):

	EXTRA-LIGHT	LIGHT	MEDIUM	HEAVY
1st	.010	.012	.013	.014
2nd	.014	.016	.017	.018
3rd	.022	.025	.026	.028
4th	.030	.032	.035	.038
5th	.038	.042	.045	.048
6th	.048	.054	.056	.058

PICKS

Whether or not you use picks, and what kind you use, are matters of personal preference. It's a good idea, though, to have a working knowledge of both flatpicks and fingerpicks, so let's talk a little about them here.

The flatpick (plectrum) is probably the most widely used aid to playing folk guitar. With it, you can strum full chords in a rhythmically solid pattern, or pick individual notes with sharp definition. You can get the boom-chicka boom-chicka sound of Jimmy Rodgers or Woody Guthrie, or the dazzling display of single-string runs as played by Doc Watson or Clarence White. The pick enhances the sound of the guitar by giving it greater volume and a clear, sharp, ringing tone.

There are dozens, perhaps hundreds, of kinds of picks available—plastic, nylon, tortoiseshell, cellulose, metal, bone—and they come in a wide variety of shapes, sizes, and gauges. By far the most popular and widely used are the teardrop plastic kinds. They can be found in any music store, and are cheap (usually three for a quarter). Once again, the type you use will depend on how you play, the sound you like, the shape of your hand, and so on. Some picks are very large, others almost microscopic; some are long and skinny, or S-shaped; others have a hole in the middle, or a piece of cork glued to one side as a grip. The only way to find out which to use is to try them all and see which feels best. If you are doing a lot of fast, single-string work in the treble, you might want a thin, light pick, but if you are into heavy rhythm and bass work you will want something harder. I like to use a medium-gauge pick, but I try to find picks that are a little on the thin side for added flexibility.

The pick is held between the thumb and forefinger, but not gripped too tightly. Although there are as many ways of holding the pick as there are pickers, the most usual way to start is: Hold your right hand in a relaxed way so that your fingers are curled halfway between open and closed. Lay your thumb gently on the side of your index finger so that the outside edges of your first thumb joint is about even with the first joint of your index finger. Now slide your pick between your thumb and index finger with the point perpendicular to your index fingernail. How much of the point you want sticking past your finger will be up to you, and as you experiment you'll find the right position. The pick should strike the strings as perpendicularly as possible. It may take some practice before you can get sharp, clean notes and easy-sounding chords. Try to control the pick so you aren't playing too loudly, especially when strumming the chords.

Listen as much as possible to the great flatpick country guitarists so that you can familiarize yourself with the sound and style of flatpicking. Some required listening: Doc Watson, Clarence White, George Shuffler, Russ Barenberg, Dan Crary, Dave Bromberg. There are also a number of flatpick instruction books available.

If you play fingerstyle guitar, you should try using fingerpicks. They usually consist of a plastic thumbpick and two metal fingerpicks that fit over the tips of your index and middle fingers. Although very cumbersome at first, fingerpicks can be very helpful once you get used to them. They allow you to obtain greater volume, sharper notes, and less wear and tear on your fingers. Many of the leading fingerpickers, including Brownie McGhee, Merle Travis, the late Rev. Gary Davis, and Leo Kottke use fingerpicks to get the sound they like.

When using fingerpicks, the thumb usually plays the four bass strings, although quite often the index finger comes up and plays the G or even the D string. Some guitarists get fast runs and a tremolo effect by alternately playing on the same string with the thumb and index finger. Rev. Gary Davis played some great licks by using this technique. Again, the word is *experimentation*. Get some picks and try them out, using every combination and technique you can think of. Once you've mastered them (which will take some time) you can decide whether or not you want to use them.

Personally, I usually use my bare fingers when I pick, but I always have a set of fingerpicks in my pocket for those times that I want a stronger sound, or when I break a picking nail.

GUITAR PICKUPS

During the late Sixties, many folk guitarists switched over to electric guitars, partly because the electric provided the volume and clarity they needed in a band situation, and partly because they liked the combination of folk-type music with the contemporary electric sound.

Many folk musicians want a basically acoustic sound, but with the volume of an electric. So, they continue playing their flat-tops but add one of an assortment of guitar pickups, which are getting better and more sophisticated all the time. These pickups fall into three basic categories; the older soundhole pickup, the contact mike, and the transducer.

The most well-known old-style pickup is the DeArmond, which is similar in its technical aspects to the electronics found in most electric guitars. It usually clips into the soundhole and has magnetic coils that convert string vibration into electronic signals.

A contact mike is actually a small microphone that works on the following principle: Sound waves are sent through a diaphragm and converted into an electronic signal which is then amplified back into sound. They are conveniently small, and can attach directly to the instrument. Of the many types on the market, the most efficient is also the most expensive (naturally!).

The transducer, which is the most recent development in acoustic sound reproduction, converts sound waves directly into electronic signals. They work best when used with a preamp, which boosts the signal before it is amplified (by a guitar amp) and gives a cleaner, more powerful sound. The transducer itself is a small rectangular or round device that is usually placed on the face of the guitar, and

is held on by a special glue or wax provided by the manufacturer. The individual player must experiment with its placement to find where it sounds best for his instrument and style. The transducer may also be permanently installed on the underside of the face once the correct spot is found on the top. This installation should be performed by a professional repairman.

The most well-known brands are Buffalo, Barcus-Berry, and FRAP (Flat Response Audio Pickup). Buffalo and Barcus-Berry are single transducers that can be purchased with or without a preamp. The FRAP is actually three transducers in one device. It must be purchased with a preamp that is constructed of heavy-duty stainless steel to take the hard knocks of the road. It is considerably more expensive than the others. In general, the more you spend, the more efficient your sound reproduction will be.

THE SOUND SYSTEM

One vital piece of equipment for any performer is the means by which he projects his voice and guitar to his audience. It is essential to the success of his performance that this be done with a minimum of distortion, feedback, and other extraneous noise, while amplifying the sound with balance, clarity, and strength. A poor sound system can ruin an otherwise fine performance, and it can be a frustrating experience for both the audience and the performer.

One answer to this problem is to have your own sound system, but unless you are doing very well (or have a heavy backer) this will probably be out of your financial range. Sound systems are usually large and heavy, and you will also need someone to run and maintain it, and the means of transporting it from gig to gig. Besides, you will be giving up one of the distinct advantages of being an acoustic act—lightness and mobility. The main advantage of having your own system is that you know exactly what you have, and can perform with the assurance that your music will get across intact.

A complete sound system is made up of several components, which include microphones, a mike mixer, a power amp, and speakers. Within this framework, systems can differ in size and capability, depending on how big a space needs to be filled with sound. There are small, portable units, such as the Shure Vocalmaster, which are designed for small clubs or auditoriums of about 200 seats. There are also monstrous systems with enormous mixing boards and power to fill giant stadiums. As an acoustic act, it is doubtful that you will need anything of that magnitude unless you became a superstar—but then you wouldn't have to concern yourself with choosing a sound system anyway.

A small, portable system is very handy to have for small jobs. They fit nicely into a station wagon or a van and can be carried around without too much difficulty. The Shure system, for example, consists of a combination mixer/power amp and two column speakers about four feet high. It's a fairly easy unit to carry, and it provides an acceptably clean, if not overwhelmingly powerful, sound. Such systems are especially useful for a small group or even a solo guitarist/singer since they will normally feature six microphone inputs for vocals, and give you reverb, tone, and volume controls on each channel. A system of this type will cost anywhere from $200.00 to $1,000.00.

If you don't have a sound system of your own, it will be important when booking a gig to make sure that your employer provides a high-quality PA (public address) system. [See section on contracts for additional information.] Find out what the house system consists of, including the number of microphones, the power of the amplifier, and the size of the speakers. Naturally, the adequacy of the system will be determined by the size of the room, so you'll have to get that information as well.

If your booking is in a fairly reputable club or concert hall, chances are it will have an adequate system, especially if "name" performers play there. If it is a college, theater, ballroom, etc. then you'd better find out *in advance* what they've got.

There's nothing worse than arriving at a hall for a sound check to find that the one microphone (c. 1928) has a short, and the speakers sound like a 747 coming in for a landing in the fog.

In most contemporary concert situations, the promoter or manager of the club or theater will hire a sound company to provide and run the PA system. This is the best possible situation for all parties, since both the performers and the booker know that the responsibility for the sound production has been taken off their shoulders. Sound companies are a major part of the music business today, and they can be found in just about every part of the country. Usually operated by sound engineers with a great deal of expertise, they are equipped to handle just about every situation that could arise. They also know from experience the needs of the performer, and will do everything they can to help him out, provided the performer cooperates.

The sound company is hired at the promoter's expense in most cases, and this fact should be clearly stated in the contract. There have been times, though, that I have been uneasy about the existing sound system in a place I was going to play, and arranged for my own sound company to come in at my own expense, to insure decent sound for my show. Depending on the size of the job, sound systems can cost anywhere from $100.00 to $1,500.00 per show (and more of course for the giant stadiums and festivals), but at times they are indispensible to a secure and good sounding performance.

It is absolutely necessary to arrange for a *sound check* before each performance. You can arrange this through the booking agent or representative of the place in which you are going to play, or directly with the sound people. It should be understood by all parties that the room will be available at least two hours before the concert is due to begin, and that the sound people will set up their equipment in plenty of time for you to have a trial run-through. You should also arrange it so that the audience is not allowed in until the sound check is completed. (There is nothing worse than trying to get your sound together while your audience is arriving, and it takes the edge off of their experience as well.)

During the sound check you can test the mikes, making sure that the system is operating correctly and that you are getting the best vocal and guitar sounds possible. If you are playing in a group, you'll have to get the right tone and balance on each instrument, and run through some songs so the sound crew will know how to mix your sound. Monitors (small speakers facing you so you can hear yourself) should be adjusted and set so that there is no feedback. The crew will adjust the height and positioning of each microphone so that you can come out and play without having to reposition or fiddle with anything during your show. All of these things will take time and effort, but the results will be worth it. Your

sound will be as professional as possible.

With some experience, you will become proficient at what is called *mike technique*. You will know how close to sing so as not to distort your sound, or drown someone else out. You'll learn to "work the mikes" by playing closer or further away to get particular sounds, and you'll know which types of mikes you should stand away from and which kinds you should "eat," singing so close your lips are practically touching them. If you play an amplified instrument, you'll learn how to avoid getting shocks (which everyone gets at one time or another, on his lips, nose, or hands) while in the middle of a performance. These are all techniques that you learn with time and experience, but it is essential that you know at least what to expect, and to set high standards for your sound and the equipment that produces it.

HOYT AXTON

WHERE TO PLAY

ELIZABETH COTTEN

Okay. Now you can play, you have a repertoire, and are outfitted with all your equipment. That part is the easiest part. Now you've got to take them out and make a living. Not so easy.

There are many places to play: roadhouse bars; folky coffee houses; night-clubs; community concerts; benefits; open-air festivals; ski resorts; summer camps and resorts; college folk clubs; concerts in large universities and major cities. The problems are: how to get to the places you want to play, and how to get your act together in such a way that you will be hired to play other, better and higher-paying places.

CLUBS

Usually when you are just starting out, you look green (both literally and figuratively), partly from stage fright or general discomfort, and partly from inexperience. Your stage presence grows as your self-confidence grows, and the audience usually knows it. These growing pains are something we all go through, and you should try to keep in mind that experience is something you earn, and it will come in time if you keep working at it.

The first thing you have to do, in many places, is audition for a job. This is one of the most painful experiences you will have to endure as a performer. I can remember several times standing on the stage of an empty nightclub or auditorium, with the boss sitting there looking bored, a "show me" attitude in his eyes. I nervously tried to rouse some spirit from my sweating hands and shakey voice, and seriously considered junking my guitar that very day.

Certain places have eased, if not eliminated, that predicament by holding their auditions on special nights reserved for "showcasing" new talent, and (although the meat rack feeling is still retained to some extent) it is offset by the atmosphere and enthusiasm of the audience. This type of showcasing began as "Hootenanny Night" at New York's Bitter End and Gerde's Folk City. And the idea of a "new talent" night appealed to all parties: performers who needed a place to be heard or try out new material, while at the same time gaining valuable stage experience; club owners who could fill their room with eager young talent (during its heyday, Gerde's Folk City made more money on their Monday "Hoots" than any other night of the week) and pull in enormous crowds to see them; record company scouts, managers, and agents keeping up with a fast-moving scene; journalists trying to get a scoop on the latest young star being born. (Actually, the only ones who have been actively against such showcases are the unions, who feel that the showcases exploit the musi-

cians and put otherwise paid members out of work. But the unions have rarely done anything about the showcases, probably because they also see the benefits of such a system.) The early and mid-Sixties were the highpoints of showcasing in folk clubs, when Dylan, Paxton, Ochs, Joni Mitchell, and other young stars would make frequent appearances, but the showcase concept is still flourishing in many parts of the country and still fulfilling the same function it did ten years ago.

Outside of the main cities, club gigs are not a very satisfying way to launch a career, but they can keep a group or a soloist working (and eating) for some time. In the upstate New York area where I live, there are several roadside bars in which 'live' music competes with the jukebox, tinkle of glasses, ringing cash register, and the resident rowdies and drunks. Still, there are many people who enjoy hearing 'live' music and I know a few groups who make a steady (though poor) living making the rounds of the taverns with names like Rosa's Cantina, Frivolous Sal's and Edgar's Disco. The most acceptable type of music for these places, aside from loud rock or innocuous cocktail music, is bluegrass and country. And this is the successful sound in bars and taverns all across the country. While these jobs can keep a group alive (barely), and can give a group solidity and stage presence through the experience of constantly playing to a tough audience, they are a dead-end as far as a wider career in the music business goes. Eventually, you'll have to step out into something else.

A definite step up the ladder are the small coffee houses and folk clubs that seem to exist in most college towns and larger cities. The audience is usually (though not always) interested in the music, and the vibes are much better, especially if you are into more personal, quiet music. You can also start building up a steady audience for later on. If you are completely unknown it may be difficult to get a job at first, but with persistence you can do "guest sets" or "opening act" shows until you are recognized and hired on your own. If you develop a good local reputation, you can go back every few months for better money each time, and after a while even small clubs of this kind will pay $100 per night. If you get a good route established, say within a 200-mile radius of your home town, you can do all right financially and start building up your audience for later concerts and recordings. If you live anywhere near a large university, check out their Student Activities Office about a possible folk club or coffee house.

There are several clubs across the country that are small, folk-oriented, and attract a serious, dedicated following. These clubs have become nationally famous because of the taste and talent of their performers. These places usually serve coffee and fancy teas, exotic pastries, and ice cream sundaes, and charge a modest admission fee. The performer usually gets a small guarantee against a percentage of what comes in at the door. The size of the guarantee and the percentage are often negotiable, depending on the drawing power of the artist. I have played at many of these places and have always enjoyed myself because of the quality of the audience, the intimate atmosphere, and the general good vibes surrounding the performance. I have probably averaged about $200 per night in these small coffee house/folk clubs, although it varies a great deal depending upon the weather conditions, my reputation in a particular area, how often I've played there, etc. Some of the most well-known clubs of this type, both for high-quality folk music and good performing atmosphere are: The Cafe Lena, Saratoga Springs, New York; The Town Crier Cafe in Beekman, New York; The Ark in Ann Arbor, Michigan; The Quiet Knight in Chicago; Freight And Salvage, Berkeley, California; and many others too numerous to list.

I mentioned college folk clubs and coffee houses—some years ago students started to requisition their school cafeterias, rathskellers, snackbars, and lounges, turning them into weekend folk clubs. Such clubs have proliferated, and some of them have achieved the status and reputation of the regular commercial clubs. Since they are occasionally subsidized by the school's Student Activities budget, they can guarantee a larger amount, or sometimes offer a flat fee that is better than anything you can get at a comparable place elsewhere. Although the pay scale, as in commercial places, is directly related to your fame or drawing power, these clubs can start as low as $75 a weekend, but go as high as $1,500 for a name act.

Another type of place to look into, if you are in the right area for it, is the ski resort, many of which have weekend entertainment. The crowds here are not serious listeners, but are usually sociable and friendly. I have a friend who makes most of his year's living touring the ski places in Vermont for a few months each winter. There are side benefits too—you might learn to ski. Watch out for broken arms or legs, which are not healthy for guitar players (or normal people either). Again, you might have to audition for a gig at one of these resorts, although a good recommendation might do as well.

The most important place for a newcomer to make a name on any large scale is in the more commercially successful, big-operation clubs. Most of these have made their reputations over the years by booking solid, big-name performers and by having owner/managers with a strong business sense. Many musicians have made great successes from appearing in these clubs two or three times a year, building their reputations from the press and recording contacts they've made from these gigs. A club like this usually has a "listening room," set up as a combination cabaret/theater, with a restaurant and bar as part of the operation. The best of them are well-run, with top-quality sound systems, theatrical lighting boards, and high-quality commercial entertainment. Although most of these clubs now run an eclectic program combining rock, folk, soul, comedians, and country music—in fact, anything that's currently commercial—many started out as straight folk clubs during the Sixties, and made their names with popular acts as

Peter, Paul And Mary; Tom Paxton; Ian And Sylvia; and The Clancy Brothers. The Bitter End in New York, The Troubadour in Los Angeles, The Cellar Door in Washington, and The Main Point in Philadelphia have all been known as "folk clubs" and have been very successful through the years.

Naturally, someone just starting his career will find it difficult to get a booking in a club of this type, although there are opportunities to get exposure as an "opening act" or warm-up for the headliner. You get little pay, but it is an opportunity to play for a knowledgeable audience that may include press reviewers, record company people, agents, or just people in "the business" who will be helpful for you to meet. Before you try it, though, be sure you've got your act together!

Unfortunately, many of these clubs have become such big business in recent years that they are often controlled by record company/agency tie-ins that make it impossible to play without a record to plug or a manager or agency with a little muscle. Many times an agency will include an unknown as part of a package with a star, forcing the club to take him even if they've never heard of him. [See section on agencies for more details.] Clubs often are so important as a way of exposing an artist that record companies have been known to *pay* a club to take their artist for a week, although the act was not sufficiently known to bring in any customers. The act's name in the papers and possible reviews in connection with a "name" club would do his career and record some good.

As an opening act in a good club you can expect to make a flat fee of $200 to $500 for a five- or six-night week, usually playing two shows on weeknights and three on the weekend. The headliner will usually get a flat fee ($1,500 and up) against a percentage, which means that everything above an agreed-upon amount that comes in at the door (admission charge) will be split between the club and the performer. This percentage will depend upon how successfully the performer's agent can negotiate, but the split may be 50% or even 60% of the

gate for the performer, which means that a popular act in a good club can make $5,000 or more per week.

I have been burned (not paid) only a few times in my career, and two of the most memorable happened at clubs. The first time was in Toronto in 1963 after a group I was playing with had finished a two-week engagement at a fancy nightclub. The owner was to drive us to the airport, and on the way stop at the bank to deposit some cash and get us a check for $600. He was late picking us up, and we sped to a bank, got the check, zoomed off to the airport and barely caught the flight to New York with guitars, banjos, and suitcases flying behind. It wasn't until we took off that we discovered that our hard-earned "check" was really a deposit slip from the bank, and completely useless to us. By the time the musicians' union took up the matter, the club was sold to someone else, and we couldn't collect.

The last time was ten years later at a Miami "folk club." By this time I was performing with my brother Artie and we were getting deposits (50% in advance), so it wasn't as bad as it might have been. Even so, when we arrived the day after closing to get our check, the place was padlocked for good and the owner had skipped town. Of course, he never even hinted that he was closing shop, and he obviously never intended to pay us the full amount of our contract.

Fortunately, these cases are the exception, and although every performer has stories about getting burned in the various devious ways, most club owners are straight about paying, and will give you the full amount in cash after the last performance. They know that if they want to stay in business, the good name and reputation of their club is essential to getting the performers they want. If you have any doubts, ask for advances after each show in the amount that would be due you at that point. A 50% deposit upon signing the contract is not an unreasonable demand, although many clubs will not do that.

One minor point that might be of help:

When you start work at a club with a bar, establish with the owner what the club's policy is on liquor tabs. Sometimes a club will give a half-price on food and liquor to performers and their guests, sometimes food is free but not drinks, and other times beer and wine are free but liquor is full-price. If you are on your own there won't be too much of a problem, but if you have a group with you, and you have a bar tab (charge account) you may end up spending more money on drinks than you make in salary. It can be a real shock when you go to collect your check and you find out that *you* owe *them* money!

CONCERTS

The most lucrative area for playing is in concerts, especially if you are able to string several dates together in a fairly short amount of time. Concerts are generally one-night stands in auditoriums, theaters, or gymnasiums (the worst places in my opinion) as opposed to a nightclub or cabaret format, which usually entails several nights or weeks in one place. Concerts are produced at many different levels, from small 100-seat rooms to elegant halls, including the recent phenomenon of playing in gigantic arenas, stadiums, and racetracks. Concerts are generally produced in one of two ways: by independent entrepreneurs who promote concerts as a (hopefully) profit-making business; and colleges and universities that produce concerts by and for the benefit of the students. I'll explain the way each one functions.

COLLEGE CONCERTS

The college and university circuit has long been the mainstay of performing musicians, making up a large percentage of their annual income. There are an enormous number of such institutions, and in certain parts of the country a

musician can do very well by performing within a 200- to 300-mile radius of his home. In the New York/New England area, for instance, there are dozens of city and state universities, junior colleges, community colleges, as well as the private colleges and universities. These schools usually provide a substantial budget to student committees of various kinds to produce musical concerts, workshops, festivals, and other programs. I have played in classrooms, in small "lounge" concerts, and student coffee house concerts (mentioned above), usually for modest but decent pay ($75 to $250); medium-sized auditoriums with good acoustics and attentive audiences (averaging about $750); and larger auditoriums and mammoth gyms with "name" acts and thousands of students sitting in bleachers and on the floor (depending on the popularity of your act, the price for these concerts can range from $500 to $10,000). The pay for these concerts is always reliable, although as a precaution I have always insisted on a deposit in advance and payment by a school (or certified) check.

Until quite recently the funds for these concerts came directly from a student activities fees, which each student was required to pay along with his tuition. With several thousand students paying these fees, the amount that a university could put into an annual entertainment budget was quite substantial, enough to provide top-flight entertainment while practically subsidizing certain areas of the performing arts. As of this writing, things have changed somewhat, for two reasons. The first is the economic crisis that is affecting both higher education facilities and the economy as a whole. Schools are tightening their belts, paying less, having less entertainment, and taking fewer chances on unknown or experimental performing arts. Students or committees in charge of entertainment now have to break even, or show a profit, on musical events to subsidize other cultural activities and bolster their deficit in other, unrelated areas. The pressure that this puts on the booking committees can turn students into profit-seeking, deal-making promoters, rather than creative people looking for a wide cross-section of artistic expression in the schools.

The major result of the economic pressure is that lesser-known folk musicians or performers who do not cater to the 'hit' mentality of pop music are being overlooked in favor of sure-fire rock and roll stars. If a school has a $20,000 budget, for instance, they will usually prefer to have two $10,000 acts per year and thereby guarantee a crowd and a profit, rather than ten $2,000 acts that are not so profitable to the school even though these acts provide a variety of music and more intimate contact between performers and audience.

It is difficult to get college concerts nowadays without a current record or a manager or agent who works with the school, unless you've made a local reputation in the area and the students know you. The best entry into the lower rungs of this scene is your record—even if it is produced on a small label. The student/promoter can use it on the campus radio station for promotion purposes, and tie-ins can be made with the local record stores (blatant commercialism, but thought of as a wise business move).

If you are unknown to the college scene, the next-best thing to a record would be to send a tape of your music or try doing guest sets at campus coffee houses or local festivals. Occasionally a school will hire an act they think is worthy of being heard by large numbers of people, putting them on as opening act to a visiting performer. This situation has many advantages although there are distinct disadvantage as well: When the audience has paid to hear their favorite act, the warm-up had better be good, or the crowd can be very difficult to contend with—especially if several members of the college audience have been consuming wine and/or drugs and are ready to "boogie."

I have had one memorable experience at a folk festival at a college in New Hampshire. It took place in the field house, a kind of indoor football field, and the crowd was latter-day Neanderthal. Beer cans were sailing across the room and occasionally landing on the stage, and the kids were dancing even when there wasn't any audible music. We followed Dave Van Ronk, and came on singing our usual up-tempo, good-time music. After two songs, though, we were so brought down that Artie and I just looked at each other wondering whether to walk off or stay. We finished our set by singing the quietest, most spiritual songs we knew, not even trying to get the crowd more riled up than they were anyway. We weren't exactly the hits of the night, but we satisfied some strange aesthetic sense in ourselves, and several people told us later that our attitude and performance were much appreciated. But, were we glad to get off that stage!

Trying to book yourself into these scenes can be a frustrating and exasperating business. It puts you in the embarrassing position of having to sell yourself, blowing your own horn, bickering over price, and generally putting yourself in an unfavorable light with your prospective employers. This is where the advantages to having an agent or manager come in, as you will see in a later chapter.

NATIONAL EDUCATIONAL CONFERENCE

If you are booking yourself without the aid of an agent or manager, this is an organization you should know about. The NEC is a nationwide association of colleges dedicated, in part, to bringing college representatives and performers together. It also, supposedly, maintains a high level of standards, rating performers for the sake of the college bookers in a monthly newsletter and an annual yearbook. (Unfortunately, they don't rate the colleges for the performers. I would like to know the working conditions in a school before I travel several hundred miles to perform there.) The NEC does provide a unique service, and they provide valuable information such as the names and addresses of schools, and who to contact for bookings. In addition, the NEC puts on regional and national conferences, which are the college entertainer's version of industrial sales convention exhibits. Booths are set up by agencies, managers, and individual performers, and each exhibitor is allowed a certain number of acts to perform. The commodity at these conventions is music rather than eggs or refrigerators, but they are useful nevertheless. If a performer does really well at a conference, he is usually signed up for a large number of well-paying jobs right there. It is usually the high-charged energy groups that tickle the fancy of the student "buyers," though, and a solo guitarist or folk singer is not likely to do well in that atmosphere. Still, participating in the NEC affair brings him to the attention of the students, and he will likely get a better reception the next time he or his representative calls the Student Activities Office for a gig.

It costs $75 per year to belong to the NEC, but participation in the regional or national conferences costs an additional fee, so you've got to be willing to invest some money in this scene.

COMMUNITY CONCERTS

Outside of the colleges and universities, the major sources of concert work are private promoters or, to a lesser extent, folklore organizations. The promoter will hire the hall, take care of tickets, promotion, sound, and lights. The performer is paid either a flat fee or, more usually, a smaller guarantee against a percentage of the gross take. (As in the folk club·scene described below, the better your name and reputation, the bigger your percentage.) The headliner will almost always be on the percentage, with the opening act on a flat fee and occasionally a bonus if the house is full and the concert is an unqualified financial success. This will all be negotiated beforehand by the artist or his representatives.

Concerts can come in all shapes and sizes. In New York, for instance, there are a number of small concerts produced by folk music enthusiasts in various parts of the city: The New York Folklore Center; The Pinewoods Club of the Country Dance Society; The Guitar Workshop in Long Island; The South Street Seaport (museum); among others. These concerts are low-budget operations, usually held in churches, school auditoriums, Y's, and even private homes; but the audiences are always interested and enthusiastic. The work is done by volunteer labor, and the pay, although not much by commercial standards, is usually a good percentage of the door. There is room for concerts of this type all over the country, and all it takes is enthusiasm and some effort to get a concert series together in any community. Talent can be drawn from both local and outside sources, and such concerts provide exposure for local musicians and at the same time bring new ideas and musical experiences into the community.

Folklore groups in many cities put on monthly concerts, often emphasizing traditional performers. But occasionally they will produce a solo or group concert for "new faces." Try checking out folklore groups in your area, such as those on the following list.

FOLK MUSIC SOCIETIES

State	City	Society
AL	Huntsville	Huntsville Association of Folk Musicians
AR	Mountain View	Rackensack Folklore Society
AZ	Phoenix	Phoenix Folk Arts Society
CA	Fresno	Fresno Folk Music Society
	Los Angeles	Southern California Folklore Society
	San Francisco	San Francisco Folk Music Club
CO	Denver	Denver Friends of Folk Music
CT	New Haven	New Haven Folk Society
DC	Washington	Folklore Society of Greater Washington
IL	Chicago	University of Chicago Folklore Society
IN	Bloomington	Hoosier Folklore Society
KY	Bowling Green	Kentucky Folklore Society
LA	Mamou	Louisiana Folk Foundation
	New Orleans	Louisiana Folklore Society
MA	Boston	The Boston Area Friends of Bluegrass and Old-Time Music
MI	East Lansing	East Lansing Friends of Folk Music
	Kalamazoo	Kalamazoo Folklife Society
MS	Decatur	Mississippi Folklore Society
NC	Raleigh	North Carolina Folklore Society
NE	Lincoln	American Old-Time Fiddler's Association
NJ	Maplewood	Folk Music Society of Northern New Jersey
NM	Gallup	New Mexico Folklore Society
NY	Albany	Pickin' 'n' Singin' Gatherin'
OH	Bowling Green	Ohio Folklore Society
PA	Philadelphia	Philadelphia Folk Song Society
TN	Murfreesboro	Tennessee Folklore Society
TX	Austin	University Folklore Association
WA	Seattle	Seattle Folklore Society
WI	Madison	University of Wisconsin Folk Arts Society

The above list illustrates how wide-spread the folksong movement still is. The list may not apply to the area where you live, but with a little searching you should find an active group nearby.

As with the club scene, finding work at larger, commercial concerts may be difficult unless you already have a name and a following, or have a strong manager or agent with some pull. Then you may be able to get on a show as an opening act or as a "special guest" as they sometimes euphemistically call a lesser-known performer.

BENEFITS

Folk musicians have long been associated with social movements and "causes," so when funds are needed the first thing most organizers think of is a folk concert. As someone who has played in hundreds of benefits, I can tell you that there are very good things about making yourself available for these concerts, providing they are well run, that you agree with their purposes, and that money is actually made for the causes to be benefited.

The primary reason for playing in a benefit concert is to make a contribution to something you believe in, and to make public your feelings about a particular issue. Sometimes you may be helping to raise money for a civic organization, hospital, or other community effort; sometimes you may be taking a controversial political or social stance that will put your life and reputation on the line (really!). Your participation then is an act of speaking out, and by your appearance you are standing up for something you believe in.

There is a more mercenary consideration: Many well-known folksinger/guitarists have made their reputations playing in benefit concerts, and have themselves benefited by receiving offers for paying gigs or record contracts as a result of being seen in such concerts. These are also excellent outlets for getting valuable stage experience, and some audiences can be very challenging indeed. I mentioned earlier my first experiences playing for hospitals and homes. These were very rewarding but difficult times; they taught me valuable lessons about *communicating* as well as making good music, and about relating to people from a stage and breaking down the mental or physical barriers between us. Other benefits I have played have ranged from cocktail parties for political candidates to mass marches against the Vietnam War. Some of the rallies and concerts I have played were terrifically exciting, and some were poorly organized, ill-conceived, drawn-out bores. Still, I don't think I've ever regretted doing benefits for things I've believed in, and I will continue to do them as long as they seem sincerely motivated and relatively well put together.

Whenever I am asked to do a benefit, and I agree with the cause, I ask certain questions before committing myself to appearing: What other performers or speakers are definitely line up? How many people does the hall seat, and how much is the admission? What is the probability of the show making money? If you are playing for little or no money, you'll want to be fairly certain that it will not be for nothing. It is very discouraging when the organization or individual is not helped by your time and effort. Make sure that the concert is being produced by competent people who know how to get a decent PA system, good publicity, a well-organized concert hall, and a good stage manager or MC to keep the show moving well. Find out exactly where the profits are going, and how they are being handled.

I usually ask for a small amount of money to cover expenses or as a small "honorarium" which, although no more than a token fee, puts me on a professional basis with the organizers. You'd be surprised at the difference this can make in the way you are regarded and treated by those in charge. This fee can be as low as $15 or as high as $100, depending on the circumstances. Always state your fee, no matter how small, before you agree to the concert, so that the folks you're playing for know what to plan. Later, if you see that the concert hasn't made much money, you can always waive the fee.

FESTIVALS

The day of the big folk festival seems to be over, but there are still many around that are worth taking in, either as a performer or as a spectator. Each festival that I have been to has had its own peculiar atmosphere and style. Some are small and community/family oriented, others large and wide-ranging in musical styles and tastes; still others are specialized, focusing exclusively on one type of music, such as blues, bluegrass, old-time mountain music, international folklore, or fiddle music. Aside from the advantage of hearing many different musicians at the same place in one weekend, the best of the festivals have the added appeal of being a meeting ground for amateurs and professionals alike. It is often possible to meet and pick with excellent musicians, and to hear top players jamming among themselves, often producing the most inspired music you will ever hear. Since festivals rarely pay well, musicians appear for two main reasons: to get needed exposure to large, enthusiastic audiences; and to meet and pick with their colleagues. There can be a wonderful feeling of camaraderie in the onstage or backstage partying and picking.

Many festivals have a "new talent" or "young folks" concert, and the producers or festival committees are usually open to audition tapes, records, recommendations, and, occasionally, 'live' auditions. Bluegrass festivals usually have banjo, fiddle, guitar picking, and other contests for amateur or semi-professional musicians—there is even a flatpicking championship at one of the bluegrass festivals (Winfield, Kansas). I suspect that the chances to compete in the guitar contests will continue to grow at these

affairs, and those who do well can usually be expected to participate actively in future festivals.

Most of the festivals that are held throughout the country are listed in the folk and bluegrass magazines. *Pickin'* (1 Saddle Road, Cedar Knolls, NJ 07927) features an annual festival guide in their spring issue, covering every kind of folk, old-time, bluegrass, and country and western festival, large or small, throughout the U.S. and Canada. Other sources of information on festivals are *Sing Out!* (270 Lafayette St., New York, NY 10001), *Bluegrass Unlimited* (Box 111, Broad Run, VA 22014) and *Muleskinner News* (Rte. 2, Box 304, Elon College, NC 27244), which publishes an annual "Bluegrass Summer" issue on festivals.

SONNY TERRY AND BROWNIE McGHEE

GETTING BOOKED

DAVID BROMBERG

I t's very helpful, and in certain circumstances necessary, to have a manager, agent, or both, particularly if you are planning to build a career in which you are in contact with a mass audience. Many bookings, especially those for recording sessions, large concerts, TV, and major clubs are virtually impossible to obtain without professional representation. Before we go any further, let me get you straight on the different types of professional representatives you might need to know.

MANAGERS

A *personal manager* is someone whom you hire to oversee your career. He is supposedly a shrewd businessman (which you assumedly are not) who will give you advice, and suggestions on your musical and business direction, stage appearance, and personal life; he will make contacts, acting for you as a go-between with record companies and booking agencies; he will set up publicity, build your public image, and in the best of the circumstances, he will be a trusted confidant and friend. He may also provide office space and bookkeeping and accouting services (often for an additional fee). For all these services he will take anywhere between 10% and 25% of your *gross* earnings.

For some time, we were working with a large, successful management firm in New York. In many ways it was helpful to have the facilities and services that our manager was able to provide. If we were on tour, the office would take care of our itinerary, keep track of the checks, make sure that contracts were signed and followed, book motel, plane, and car reservations, and generally take a lot of the burden of detail work off of us. They also got us many more bookings than we could have had we been on our own, sending us to be the opening acts at shows for their more nationally famous acts, thereby getting us excellent exposure in many parts of the country. Since it was a well-established and very successful operation, they provided services that smaller outfits or single managers could not have afforded.

It is easier to get along without a manager after you've gained something of a reputation and experience, if you feel you don't need one. It also might be difficult to get a manager *before* you've established yourself to a certain extent, so you may not have a choice at the beginning anyway.

As you start to get a reputation, though, you will undoubtedly get some offers from people who want to manage you. Unfortunately, anyone can claim they are a manager, and there are many people out there looking to latch on to a good thing if they think they smell success. If you are approached by someone who wants to represent you, check them out carefully and don't sign any long-term contracts. Agree to a trial period during which time, say six months, if the relationship is not benefiting your career you can move on. Don't sign anything without a good lawyer on your side. Remember, a good personal manager can work wonders for you, but a bad one can be a scavenger and a burden for a long, long time.

Many performers feel that they don't need such expensive services, though—that they can manage their careers on their own. Often, with the help of a lawyer, they can steer themselves in the right direction, feel which moves to make and know when to make them. And they do quite well. I know of artists who have hired a lawyer specializing in the language and dealings of the music business to negotiate contracts, to keep their books, to give advice, and to provide many of the services that a manager would provide, although on a lesser scale. Most lawyers take less of a percentage of your income (usually 5%) for their services, but their function is primarily a legal one. A lawyer's most important roles will be to read the fine print of contracts (which can be just as tricky as they are reputed to be), avoid the loopholes, and interpret the contract in their client's favor. This is especially important when negotiating long-term contracts, such as record deals. It should be noted that even if you have a manager, it is a good idea to have your own, independent lawyer *not* associated with the manager, to help interpret managerial contracts and other dealings, at least initially, with your manager.

AGENTS

A manager does a great many things, but he rarely does the actual booking —in some states it's even illegal for him to do so—leaving it up to a booking agent or agency instead. An agency can be anything from an in-the-home office run by a single person with a telephone, to a large suite of expensive offices housing dozens of secretaries, agents, public relations people, advance men (who do advance publicity), and so on. The functions of the booking agency are the same regardless of the size of the operation: to secure gigs for their musicians at the highest possible fee, to issue and enforce contracts, and sometimes collect the checks. For these services, they take from 10 to 20% "off the top" (before any deductions are taken from the gross amount paid you, the performer) of anything they get for you (15% is the norm these days). If you are under an "exclusive contract," they will take a percentage of *all* your gigs, regardless of whether or not they got the job for you. An agency that has you under contract regards (or *should* regard) you as an investment, and they assume that they are helping you to build your career and are entitled to whatever you make, unless there is a definite understanding that conditions will be otherwise. Some agencies, for instance, will recognize that under certain circumstances you will have to pay a commission to another party as well (let's say an independent promoter or booker) and they might split or even defer that particular series of commissions. On the whole, though, if you are considering signing up with an agency, it will probably be as an exclusive artist to that agency, and you will be expected to pay some percentage to them on any gigs you get.

As you can see, between a manager, booking agent, and lawyer, the percentage of your earnings that goes out (off the top, remember?) starts to become formidable.

An agency is licensed by the state, and usually must be registered with the musicians' union as a bona fide artist's representative—if the act is in the union [see below]. Those requirements give the artist some protection from any irregularities in his dealings with the agent or agency, although if he is working through a reputable agency to start with, this probably won't be necessary. But save yourself a lot of headaches later; know, *before* you sign, that you are protected.

A good booking agency can be invaluable in helping an act get started, but unfortunately the bigger ones will not take on an unknown performer unless they have a recording contract or a good manager who can assure the agency that their time and money spent building up the act will be worthwhile. It's very expensive nowadays to break in a completely new act, unless there is the potential for large demand. Then the agency can easily capitalize on this potential by booking tours, TV dates, or other high-paying jobs. This is especially unfortunate because it leaves the good but less-commercial artists with difficulty finding an outlet for their music, while the agency could, if it wanted to, find the market that is needed. It is all economics though, and not music. The cost of running a large agency doesn't leave much room for chance or altruism.

Once you are signed by a good agency, you can expect a lot of help. Usually one of the agents from the office will be assigned to look after your bookings and will be available to discuss your career's direction, where you'll play, who to contact for gigs, and other details. A good agent will work very hard, showing up at important jobs, introducing you to other promoters or club owners, scheduling interviews, and so on. If this is done conscientiously and tastefully, the agency will definitely be worth its percentage.

For a folk singer or guitarist, it might be even better to have a smaller agency or single agent who understands the folk scene, likes the music, and can take a personal interest in you without the heavy investment that the major agencies automatically make. A smaller-scale agent can often act as both agent and manager (where this arrangement is legal) and can be a great help to a struggling musician. There have been several agents around the country who have started out with acts that were unknown outside of a small circle of enthusiasts and single-handedly built up their careers to national proportions. Two examples come to mind: Manny Greenhill started out in Boston producing small folk concerts for unknown artists in the area, including Joan Baez, Chris Smither, and Doc Watson; Dick Waterman has been a long-time friend, manager, and agent for several blues musicians including Skip James, Son House, and John Hurt, often going out on a limb himself to see that his clients got the deal they rightly deserved. He recently made a national name for himself with Bonnie Raitt, whom he had been managing for several years before she became a well-known artist.

The relationships between managers, agencies, and record companies can become fairly complex. It is often the manager who gets you the deal with the agency, and either the manager or agent can get you a record deal (the bigger the manager the better the deal) and the record company works with the agency on promotion so that personal appearances can be tied in to record sales. The manager will also play an important role in negotiating with the record company, both before and after the record is released, to make sure that everything possible is being done for the client.

In order to get a better picture of the role of booking agents and what they would mean to you, I spoke with Bruce Nichols, an old friend and ex-agent of mine who is now working for APA (Agency for the Performing Arts). This is one of the largest and most prestigious agencies in the country, with offices in New York, Chicago, San Juan, Miami, and Los Angeles, and whose clients are some of the biggest names in show business. Still, Bruce has consistently shown an interest in smaller-name, folk-oriented performers whom he has tried to help and develop as major artists. Some of the guitarist/singers with whom he has worked are: Brownie McGhee, Eric Andersen, Pat Sky, Artie Traum, Larry Coryell, Country Joe MacDonald, John Sebastian, and Dave Van Ronk. What follows is my conversation with Bruce.

H.T. The first thing I ought to ask you is the most obvious question: What does an agent do?

B.N. The first and most important job for an agent is to get work for the acts that he represents. Secondly, he has to find acts to represent, so he has a two-fold responsibility. An agent is actually a kind of middle man between the artist and/or the artist's manager, and the person who actually buys the talent. It is his responsibility to find the people who want the talent, negotiate a deal that is acceptable to the artist, discuss it with the artist (recommending that it be taken or not taken), until finally he issues the contracts and sees that they are fully executed. The agent will occasionally go out on a job with the artist, since it's so important for him to know what his artist is doing onstage (and before and after the performance, too) in terms of how professional he is, what kind of problems may arise, and so on. This is especially true when you first start to represent an act, since no matter how much the act may tell you about what they want, and what they plan to do when they get to an engagement, when you actually get there and see what goes down you have a much better idea of what's going on.

H.T. Do you go out on the road with the group?

B.N. You obviously want to stay in touch with an act in terms of what they're doing, so you usually see them when they are in or near the city where the agency is. We can't be on the road too much, because the agent's job is being on the telephone, and knowing what's going on with the other agents and other acts. With the exception of the biggest acts, the majority of the dates are booked by phoning people, rather than taking calls coming in. This is where most of the work is.

H.T. How would someone go about getting an agent?

B.N. I'll tell you, that's really tough, and I'll have to give you a little background about an agency to begin with. Now, I'm talking about the larger agencies that deal with substantial talent. Basically, how much an act can earn on a per-engagement basis, and how much an act can work, is based on how much exposure it's had. The largest exposure, of course, is records. For a new artist, it's very difficult to go through either the agency thing or the record company thing. Managers, record companies, and others in the business can work on a fairly high profit—(they also have a higher investment, I have to say that)—but they can make more money when it "happens" for them. An agency is restricted by The American Federation of Musicians and the other unions as to how much money they can take from an act, and when you start talking about telephone and mail costs and so forth as they are today, it just doesn't pay to book an unknown. For example, if you were doing the coffee house circuit, you may be talking about $125 to $250 a week, and it gets pretty expensive for an agency working at ten or fifteen percent to really put a lot of time, effort, and money into an act like that. So agents are generally very, very careful about what they take on in terms of acts that do not have some kind of exposure—they want to be sure that they can make some money. Records provide the biggest exposure. There's the National Entertainment Conference, which probably supplies the biggest single way to get exposure in the colleges. Of course, there's radio and television....

H.T. But you can't get these things without an agent.

B.N. You *can* get these things without an agent, but it's pretty difficult for an artist to sell himself at any time. What happens is he doesn't push hard enough to get the people really interested, or to get the kind of money that he might be able to get from a buyer. Or he pushes so hard that it sounds like he's on an ego trip. An agent or any other person representing the act—whether it's a friend who knows what he's doing, a wife, whatever—can take that pressure off the act and be able to push on something that the artist himself might not be able to do and come off well with the buyer. I think it's important to have some buffer between the artist and the buyer if at all possible. I know that's very difficult for someone just starting.

H.T. How would you recommend getting started?

B.N. The easiest way to start is in your local area. Become involved in the music scene in that area, go to the local clubs, talk to the colleges, and so forth. It might mean an exposure for free at some point—getting on a show at the local community college in front of a Tom Paxton, a Livingston Taylor, a Bromberg. That way, people will begin to know you in that immediate area. Playing the college coffee house for $5 or $50 a night or whatever it is. If it's New York City or San Francisco, there are plenty of clubs around for people to play. For the guitar player/singer, the guitar is part of him—he can't perform without it—and if he's going to drop in on a folk club in Greenwich Village or out in San Francisco, he's got to have that guitar with him. At any time he may have the opportunity to play, maybe it's only one song, but it may be important. I don't mean to make it sound easy. There are people who go in and play the showcases, for example, in clubs that have them the one night a week that would normally be their dark night. They don't pay the people, it's a cattle call, there may be thirty or forty people on in one night, doing one or two songs each, and that's it, they're off the stage. I would guess that most of the time the person who books the talent isn't even around, he's out front talking to somebody or having a drink with somebody or on the phone—maybe he took that night off because there's not a big act in there. But, the one time that the guy *is* there he may see something that he likes and ask you to come back and maybe pay special attention to you next time. I can't tell you how many times someone might have to go into a place like The Other End and play there while people are talking and drinking, but suddenly Paul Colby might become aware that there is something on the stage that is special and starts to think, "Gee, maybe I *could* put him on a show."

H.T. Then do you feel that an act should come to the big cities, or should they stay in their local areas to get started?

B.N. Well, there are two different kinds of situations. An act can be very important out in Ohio, Illinois, Indiana, without anyone in

New York or Los Angeles knowing who they are. Now eventually, if they're going to break in in a big way, they're going to have to get to those major cities, record companies, a big-time agent, etc., but local groups can make pretty good money in their own areas, and eventually they may come to the attention of the people in the larger cities. There's one problem with that. A lot of acts will start to make $1,500 to $2,000 per night in a given geographic area, and then comes the time that a record comes out and they have to move out on a national basis, and suddenly that money is not available in the national markets because they've got to be exposed in those markets before the radio stations, rack jobbers, and so on pick up on them. My advice would be: When you have not made it big, but have an area in which you are making money, don't go out and live high on that money. Put as much of that away as possible so you can begin to move into New York, Chicago, Los Angeles, or San Francisco—wherever it is that you have to go to break into the big time.

H.T. Let's say there's a young, unknown Eric Andersen who comes and knocks on your door and says, "What can you do for me?"

B.N. Obviously, if someone who is a fairly substantial figure in the music business comes to us and says, "Hey, this is a talent you ought to take a look at," that is going to mean a lot more to me than somebody whom I've never heard of before, since I know that person has a track record, and has proven his judgment by working with and developing talent over a considerable period of time. The competition is *fierce*. Normally what we do when somebody calls us or drops by, and I know it sounds like a real put-off to people, is say: "Please, before we waste your time and you waste ours, get us some product, even if it's a homemade tape." We *do* listen to it (although sometimes it takes us a couple of weeks to get to it) and we do get back in touch with the people. We may send the tape back and say, "this is very nice but there's nothing we can do at this point." We may suggest that there are people they can contact who may be interested in that

particular person, even though we're not. It may be somebody who's involved in management, publishing, a record company, whatever. We very, very seldom sign acts that do not have either a very wide recognition or a record deal. On the present list of acts that we represent, we have one act like that, whom we really believe in, with whom we are working to expose them to a larger number of record people. They write and sing in an America/Crosby, Stills, Nash vein. Now, if the major record companies come and see the act, and they're not interested, we're going to have to tell that act, "Hey, there isn't anything else we can do for you." They are on the coffee house circuit now, playing a lot of schools, but not making any money. If a record company is not going to pick them up right now, we just can't make it pay to work with them.

H.T. If someone gets signed by an agency, does that mean he's going to make more money? Would it up his price because an agent is representing him?

B.N. That's a hard question. Certainly it should over a period of time, but in some cases it may actually mean the money's going to go down. Now that's a strange thing to say, but take again that local act who signs with a major agency. They've now got to get national exposure. We've got one act now that has a very strong following in the Southwest and they make very good money, but at some point they've got to break out of that Southwestern area. Maybe the record company can do it (they've got a new album coming out) but chances are, for the record company to do their job, somebody's got to book them on a tour that's going to include places like The Bottom Line or The Other End in New York. or The Main Point in Philly, and other clubs around the country. Now they're not going to be making the kind of money they're used to in those places. But that's the step they've got to take in order to get that shot at making big money later on. On the other hand, a group might come to us who's been making $125 a week on the coffee house circuit, and we might be able to fit some dates into that tour at $500 a night. That's going to up what they're making considerably. That can make a big difference for an act in that situation. An act may come to us who's been booking itself but just hasn't known where to go, and we may be able to put them into new markets for more money. Or we may be able to get them more bookings, so even if their per-night price doesn't go up, they may gross more per week. A lot depends on the group's overhead.

H.T. Could you elaborate on that?

B.N. One thing that's nice about a singer/guitarist or a duo that doesn't have a lot of equipment is that they can move around, go where the dates are. We handle Larry Gatlin, for example, who is being widely recognized as a future superstar of country music. Our effort is to push him across that country line and into pop music because, although he comes from Nashville and has certain country mannerisms, he's not really a country singer in the traditional sense. Now, because he's a single artist with just a guitar, we may get one night in Detroit and if the next night he has to be in Los Angeles, there's no problem. You get a band with five or six people and equipment, road manager, and that kind of stuff, that type of routing is just impossible. So that's one great advantage of being a folkie.

BOOKING YOURSELF

If you don't want (or cannot get) an agency or manager to help you get gigs, you can try to do it yourself, although I know from personal experience that this can be tedious, time consuming, and often frustrating. Your expenses will be high, and you'll have to be good at getting gigs in order to justify your financial investment. Of course, the advantage is that you get everything you make, and you don't have to worry about satisfying someone else's taste or income requirements. If you are successful at it, even for a short period of time, it will feel very good.

You've got to be good, first of all, at selling yourself. If you have trouble with this, or are not aggressive on the telephone, you may want to hire someone else, either on a percentage or an hourly basis, to do that part of it for you. As I've said before, many people find it very difficult to bicker over price and have to prove their worth to some unknown person at the other end of the telephone line.

Unless people are calling you for gigs, you'll have to get them yourself, and aside from direct contact (auditions, guest sets, and other personal appearances) you'll have to do it by mail and phone. This means that you'll need something to send out and a phone (with lots of credit with the phone company).

For mailing purposes, you'll need to get a good publicity photo of yourself and a flyer or brochure that contains a short "bio" (biography), including where you've played, a general description of what you do or the kind of music you play, and any reviews you've received. The photo should be an 8x10 glossy, which you can have printed commercially for about $30 per hundred. The flyer/brochure can be very simple, but should be neat and well-designed, attractive to the eye, and easy to read. It can be typed on a good electric typewriter, or typeset professionally for not too much money. Then it can be printed by photo-offset at a good "quick-copy" printer for between $5 and $10 per hundred, or if you want a more classy job, a regular printer could do the job—but it would cost two or three times more than the "quick-copy" printer. The better it looks, though, the more easily you will impress the people in charge of bookings.

The flyers and photos should be sent (along with any more recent press clippings) to clubs, colleges, or promoters who might be looking for artists. It should be sent with a personal letter that explains why you are writing, and that you will follow the mailing with a phone call in a few days.

Be prepared for large phone bills! Unless you are working very locally, you'll be making a large number of long-distance calls that can reach astronomical proportions before long. If you are calling school committees you'll have to call person-to-person, since the person to whom you want to speak is rarely where he's supposed to be. Your calls probably won't be returned, no matter how many times you leave a message, so you'll be spending a great deal of your time on the phone. When you reach someone, they probably won't give you an answer right away, but will have to refer it to a committee, and it goes on and on this way until you finally score a gig (hopefully). It can be very frustrating, indeed.

Before you call, have a pretty good idea of what you need financially from the booking. It is a good idea, if you are in a position to do so, to set a minimum fee below which you will not play even if it means not getting a gig. This way you set certain standards for yourself, and as long as that minimum is not too outrageous, you will be respected for it.

It is a very difficult thing to work out what you think you are worth for an appearance somewhere. You will have to consider the size of the place, how far you have to travel, whether you are taking other musicians with you, your expenses to and from the gig, how much it cost you (in phone calls, publicity, etc.) to get the gig, the amount you are paying other musicians or equipment men, and finally how much you need for yourself. Let's say that after your expenses you could get by with $50 for yourself (not much considering the energy and talent you are putting out). You might have to insist on $150 in order to come out ahead. At certain times, for the benefit of your future career, you may decide to take less, but try to stick to your stated minimum price, even if it's only $50 for the whole deal. At first, try to keep your overhead to a minimum. Travel as light as possible, using only the musicians and equipment necessary to putting your talents across to the audience. This way you will keep your expenses down, too, and you will have an easier time getting the amount of money you'll need to keep yourself together.

CONTRACTS

When you are working through an agent or a manager, one of those persons will take care of all of your contracts on performing gigs. (Of course, even if someone is "taking care" of your contracts, you should know their contents.) If you are doing your own booking, you will have to get your own contract together. This contract between you and a club owner, promoter, or college can be anything from a brief letter of agreement to a multi-paged legal document. Basically, the contract must have the following information, agreed upon in writing by you (the artist) and the employer (whoever is paying you):

1. The name of the act (either you or your group's name) including, when appropriate, the names of anyone else who is part of the group.
2. The exact time and place of the gig: address, phone number, name of the employer's representative in charge and where they can be reached.
3. The number and length of sets, or the total amount of time you are expected to play.
4. The wage agreed upon, and the method of payment (certified check, cash, etc.), and when payment is to be delivered.
5. The name and title (position) of the signer of the contract.

In addition to these necessities, a contract may contain many other stipulations. For instance, if the employer is to provide a sound system, the contract should specify the exact number of mikes needed, minimum power requirements of the amplifiers, and size of the speakers. If a piano is required, it should state in writing that it will adhere to certain minimum standards (e.g. "concert grand piano tuned to A-440 onstage on the day of performance").

Every performer has his own personal requirements and the contract should specify these clearly and unequivocably, as long as they are within reasonable limits. For instance, I usually demand "a clean, private dressing room near the stage for the exclusive use of myself and my guests. Soft drinks, coffee, and other refreshments are to be provided...." More often than not I'm put in a drafty locker room in the basement of a gymnasium, but at least I can complain if it's in the contract. Other times, I am provided with fine accommodations and extravagant refreshments, including food, beer, and wine.

The most important thing is that the contract should be as specific and thorough as possible, putting in all the details that will make the job as professionally run and as comfortable for you as possible. This also helps the employer, since he knows exactly what *he* has to do in order to put on the best show he can.

The American Federation of Musicians (musicians' union) has a contract blank that must be filled out and filed with the union in order to be within their regulations (see *Unions* for more details). If you are working with an agency that is affiliated with the union, their contract will be in compliance with union regulations. Anything you'd like to add in terms of personal requirements can be added in a "rider" attached to the contract.

MERLE TRAVIS AND DOC WATSON

PUBLISHING

JONI MITCHELL

The definition of a folksinger or folk guitarist nowadays is very different from what it was a few years ago. Until recently a folksinger was someone who sang and played traditional music in a traditional, usually regional and rural, style. Today most people who consider themselves "folksingers" write much of their own material and sing and play it in a contemporary style that bears little resem-

blance to traditional folk and country sounds. The folksinger as singer/songwriter came into his own during the early Sixties when talented young poets put their expression into ballad form, performing them with guitar accompaniment. Bob Dylan, Joni Mitchell, Phil Ochs, Eric Andersen, Tom Paxton, Buffy Sainte-Marie and many others put the ideas of their time into songs. Others picked up on these songs and fitted them into their own folk-style performances; e.g. Joan Baez, Judy Collins, Tom Rush, and others who became the interpreters of the singer/songwriters.

This situation has continued to develop, bringing forth a great number of talented and successful singer/songwriters who also developed the style further afield into what, for lack of a better term, has been dubbed "folk-rock" by the music writers and critics. Paul Simon; Seals and Croft; Jim Croce; Crosby, Stills, Nash, and Young; Jackson Browne, and many others have made their music internationally famous by taking the singer/songwriter idea and adding more and more contemporary (some would say commercial) backup sounds to the basic acoustic guitar and voice format.

So today the definition of "folksinger" has changed, and many young people are writing as never before. Aside from reasons of self-expression, songwriting and publishing is where all the really big money is. An artist who sings his own songs gets many times the amount from royalties as he would if he were simply a singer. There is also the possibility that a non-writing singer will record one of the songs he hears on the album. The rewards from songwriting are so great that one song on a fairly successful album can bring in thousands of dollars, and a really big pop hit can set a writer up for life. An interesting aspect of this situation was the rush, during the "folk boom" of the late Fifties and early Sixties, for many folk groups to copyright the traditional songs they were singing and claim authorship for them. Of course, most of these songs were in the public domain (P.D.), which means anyone can make use of them without paying royalties. But millions of dollars were paid as royalties for the "arrangements" of these songs. Occasionally the real author of a song everyone thought was P.D. would surface from obscurity to collect his money, but usually the show business lawyers were too slick and these traditional writers of homemade songs ended up with the short end of the stick.

Now millionaire "folksong" writers are commonplace, and many of the songs that have been written have little to do with the struggles of everyday people. Still, there is much songwriting talent and integrity around today, and the main problem is what to do to get the new songs heard by the people who can do something with them.

COPYRIGHTS

Let's start from the beginning. Assume that you have written some songs but haven't a clue as to what to do with them. The first thing is to get them protected, and the way to do that is to secure a copyright for them. The Copyright Office at the Library of Congress in Washington, D.C. will send you forms, which you fill out and send back along with a *lead sheet* (melody line, chords, and lyrics are sufficient—carefully and neatly done), and a check or money order for $6.00 per song. Several weeks later you will receive a Notice of Copyright, which means the song will be yours for 28 years (renewable once) unless you later assign your copyright over to a publisher. In some cases your application for a copyright will be rejected either because the title, lyrics, or music are very similar to something else on file, or because you did not supply them with enough information to conduct a search. The material you send in must be written down—tapes cannot be used.

A song is also protected if it has been published in some manner, such as in a magazine, book, or record that has been copyrighted in its entirety. Just make sure that a copyright notice (in *your* name) is printed in the book or on the record. Otherwise, the copyright may revert to the publisher of the work or to their company. Your copyright notice should read:

Copyright © (year) by (your name). Used by Permission.

Another way to protect your songs, at least temporarily, is to put a lead sheet or a tape into an envelope and send it to yourself by registered mail. Do not open the envelope and you at least have proof that the song existed at a certain date. This last procedure is only a stop-gap measure, and should not be used in lieu of registering a formal copyright with the Library of Congress.

PUBLISHING

Once you have a batch of songs written and, hopefully, protected in some way, it becomes necessary to do something with them. If you sing and play your own material, the success of your songs will bear a direct relationship to the success of your career. If you are able to get a recording contract on the basis of your singing and playing, the original songs will fall right in with everything else and chances are you won't have to worry too much about them. Anyone who is a relatively successful performer, especially with a recording contract, has no trouble finding people to help them, sign them up, and help them spend their money.

However, if you are an unknown and trying to make it as a singer/guitarist, and also as a songwriter (or as a songwriter alone), you'll have to get your songs around so that they are sung and hopefully recorded. To some extent you can do this yourself, especially if you are aggressive, have good business sense, and have some contacts in the music business either with performers, artist and repertoire men (A&R men), producers or managers. These necessary qualifications are not easy to come by, but some songwriters I know have done very well by being their own agent, publisher, and "song runner." I should add, though, that this only works to a point, since if you are at all successful you will not want to be so tied up in administrative details that you no longer have time to write or sing your songs. For the most part, songwriters are more than happy to turn their material over to a publisher whose job it is to fulfill these functions.

To get a clearer picture of just what song publishers do, I went to see Linda Wortman, a New York publisher who works with such artists as Jesse Winchester, Todd Rundgren, and Bobby Charles. Our conversation follows.

H.T. What is a song publisher, and why would anyone need one?

L.W. Basically, you'd need a publisher for two reasons: The first is that when you get recorded (assuming you get a record deal) you'll need someone who is experienced in understanding all the administrative stuff in dealing with your songs. The most important reason for having a publisher, however, is to get your tunes recorded by *other* people. The main function of a professional publisher is to take the songs around and try to get people interested in them. When a song is recorded, you increase the value of the copyright, which is only a piece of paper until it generates some income.

H.T. How do you choose whose songs you're going to publish?

L.W. Obviously, if a proven writer wants me to handle his songs, there's no problem, but that doesn't happen too often. I have two guidelines: like every other publisher, I'm very interested in what people are looking for, what's happening in the business, what's on the charts, and so on because if I don't have tunes that people want to record, then I don't make sessions, which means nothing's happening. So, I'm generally looking in the ballpark of what people will consider hit material. Second, I'm looking for someone who is totally unique (which I've rarely found), totally creative, whom I'd be willing to run the risk for. I'd see if I could get him a record deal, or whatever it takes for them to be accepted. But that's the kind of thing you rarely find. It would have to be someone you'd feel was another Randy Newman, or Nilsson, or Dylan. It would have to be someone who really makes their own mark in the business.

H.T. Let's say there is that person out there in a small town in the Midwest, or in Brooklyn for that matter, who's writing songs and playing, trying to get it together. What does he do?

L.W. The first thing he has to do is come to New York or Los Angeles. He's got to put a tape together of his best material—not fifty or a hundred songs, but three to five of his absolute best, showing where this writer's most commercial stuff is at. I do see some people 'live,' but I may be one of the only publishers around who do. People walk in here with guitars and I see them, but it's rare with publishers or record companies.

H.T. When a writer gets a tape together, would it have to be a professionally recorded, slick-sounding tape?

L.W. I'm pretty good at using my imagination, but most people aren't, so don't count on that. It should be as professional as possible within the person's means. If a tape sounds really bad, most publishers are not going to listen very carefully. Nowadays, if you make a record that sounds too "folk" you're in trouble already. Even I cancel that out unless it's something incredible, because there's nothing I can do with those tunes. I can't work with them. What I'm looking for, and what I assume every other publisher is looking for, is someone who writes really good *songs*, not really good folk songs. Even the people who were singing other people's folk-type stuff a few years back—Judy Collins, Joan Baez, Tom Rush, and so on—are into more commercial material now.

H.T. What about Nashville? Aren't people doing folk-type tunes there, using steel and fiddle backup in the commercial country style?

L.W. I'm not an authority on Nashville (although I'm getting an award there for "Third-Rate Romance") but it seems to me that Nashville is changing and is going in a more commercial, pop direction. I found people were looking for tunes like the stuff coming out of Macon, such as The Allman Brothers, or else pop-country tunes. Just by adding a pedal steel to make it more commercial isn't enough from what I could ascertain.

H.T. Let's get back to that young James Taylor or Bob Dylan out there who needs to make a tape. Would it pay him to spend a lot of money on a really professional job? He'd have to hire a studio, musicians, maybe even an arranger.

L.W. I think it would pay off in the long run, but he'd have to be careful of what he's doing. He can't go chasing a wild star because he's going to become an overnight sensation. But he can produce a good tape himself. Except for the kids that have absolutely no money, the average kid today is pretty sophisticated, and you can make a good publishing demo with a 4-track Teac or something similar.

H.T. Were you saying a little while ago that the acoustic guitar sound is no longer commercially viable? There are still James Taylor; Crosby, Stills, Nash, and Young; America; and so on.

L.W. Well, it is but it isn't. How can I explain it? Loggins And Messina, America, Eagles (my absolute favorite group), are almost all acoustic and based on folk music, but they've taken it one step further. There is a market for that but unfortunately everyone's trying to copy that sound and it's pretty well saturated. What has to happen is for someone to take folk music one step more in *another* direction—I don't know the direction necessarily—but do what these people did with it. Then, *that'll* be where it's at for a while.

H.T. Okay. Let's go back again. Now that tape of the young songwriter's material is recorded. What does he do with it?

L.W. First of all, it's a total mistake to send tapes to somebody unless you know them or have some personal contact with them. What you've got to do is go to whatever city you're going to and do a little homework to find out who the publishers are, and start making the rounds. You've got to find out who screens the material, and start seeing those people. It's tough, because publishers are as choosey as the record companies are now. What happens is if the record companies are tight, so are the publishers, and they don't have the freedom to just say, "Okay, I'll take it, let's hope I get it recorded." Most publishers are only interested in people who've already recorded, since they know they'll make money off of them.

H.T. In other words, you'd need a record contract to get you an immediate publishing deal, but the publisher wouldn't necessarily get you a recording contract. So it seems that it would be better to aim first for the record.

L.W. That depends. There's an old saying that there are many ways in the door and only one way out. If you're going to go to a record company they are more than likely going to want the publishing, but then most record companies' publishing arms are not that good. They do not go out and beat the bushes the way a small independent publisher would.

H.T. Let's say someone's really good, and he gets an offer from a couple of publishers. How would he choose which was better for him? Is he going to get ripped off, or sign his life away?

L.W. At that point, he's going to have to get a lawyer, but there's no guarantee any way you look at it. In any contractual relationship, whether it's a publisher, record company, manager, booking agent, you don't really know what's going to happen. What you've got to look for is someone you feel comfortable with and that you feel can do the job for you, and whom you really think isn't snowing you, plus you should go to a lawyer. Unfortunately, most lawyers tend to do big numbers and think that each client they're negotiating for is the Beatles, so you've got to watch out that the whole thing doesn't get so involved that it gets out of hand.

H.T. What is the standard publishing deal?

L.W. There's no real "standard deal." Most publishers will want to sign for five years, but sometimes less. You'd get paid writer's royalties (mechanical royalties), which at this point means: the publisher gets paid 2¢ for every cut, out of which the writer gets a penny. If there's foreign royalty money, the writer will get half. On sheet music, the writer usually gets 6¢ a sheet, that's pretty standard. Airplay money goes directly to the writer. There are basically two performance societies, ASCAP and BMI, and when a writer becomes a member of either of these, which he does when his tunes have been recorded, then the performance society pays the publisher and the writer directly. The only way the publisher is really

involved with that is that he will take the writer to the performance society to make sure everything is registered properly, and possibly negotiate an advance (from the society).

H.T. Is it usual for a publisher to offer money to a writer for signing?

L.W. Some publishers yes, some no. I don't at this point. When you have a large publishing company that's funded by a large corporation, such as Warner Brothers Music or Screen Gems, then you have a lot of money to throw around. They can afford to take the chance of offering someone a lot of money if they think it's going to happen. It's just a tax write-off for them. A small publisher doesn't have that kind of income to work with, so what I offer as opposed to money is work, which most writers appreciate more.

H.T. What other advice can you give to people who are just starting to get into the songwriting business?

L.W. Having been in the business now for eight or nine years, I must say that it's a very rough business on any end, whether you're an executive on the top or a kid on the bottom. So, first, if you're really going to do it you've got to want to do it more than anything else in the entire universe, because it's going to involve a lot of sacrifices. Second, in order to get accepted these days, on any level, you've got to put together something that's unique, and something that can be accepted. You've got to make it incredible. Aim for the top, because if you aim for the middle it's more than likely that nobody's going to want to deal with you. When you go to a record company trying to get signed, they match you up against their best artist. If someone comes in here it's the same thing. If somebody walks in the door, he's got to be better than Jesse Winchester, or Todd, or other people I have signed here, and I don't think that's so easy. People have to realize that they've got to aim high, and they have to put together very carefully what they're doing.

RECORDING

One of the bitter truths in the world of professional music making is that it is very difficult nowadays to get any kind of a booking without a record album or "hot single" currently on the market. There was a time when clubs, colleges, or concert bookers, were actively looking for new talent that had yet to be discovered by a record label. Now, even college students are looking for "promotional tie-ins" with large companies, and the bigger clubs won't even talk to you if you are not financially supported by a label. This support can take many forms, but most often it is in "promotion"; the record company takes out large ads and performs other publicity and public relations work that would normally be on the shoulders of the club's manager if he wanted to fill his room. This also takes the form of direct payment to the club as a subsidy for a group that has questionable drawing power but needs the exposure that a good club can give it. But let's get away from the seedier side of the music business....

There are other obvious reasons for putting out a record, and fortunately the folk field holds many opportunities for deserving artists, especially in small, alternative (to the large corporations) companies. This is because the grassroots audience that supports folk music in such a dedicated way allows these low-budget, underground record companies to produce good folk, country, and blues albums. Although they don't have big money to throw around (such albums are usually made on a shoestring) and the financial rewards are not enormous, the artist almost always has direct artistic control as to what the album is all about, without consideration of saleability or mass commercial appeal. Another important reward is that small record companies keep their records in print regardless of how many they sell while the large corporate labels will allow an album to go out of print immediately if it does not turn a profit. Very often these larger labels will put albums on the market and see if their gamble on the taste of the American public pays off. If not, the record quickly becomes unavailable, the ones remaining in the stores are "remaindered," (sold at a heavy discount) and the rest are either warehoused or melted down to make other albums, as was done during the recent vinyl shortage. This means that if a record does not sell 50,000 copies, it is considered a failure. On the other hand, Folkways Records, the first and most influential record company dedicated to folk music, has over 2,500 albums out, and everyone is still in print! This is amazing, considering that some of the more esoteric albums have never sold more than a few hundred copies, but it is an indication of the dedication and belief that Folkways has in its product. This company continues to be an enormous service to anyone interested in the world's traditional music.

Although the commercial "folk boom" is long past, the major labels will still show an interest in a commercially viable folk-style performer. The continued success of Joni Mitchell, Eric Andersen, Judy Collins, John Prine, Ry Cooder, and others is an indication that there is still a market for this kind of music (although few would consider it folk in strict terms). So, although it is extremely difficult for a folk-style guitarist or singer/songwriter to get a contract on a major label, it is worth trying. The notoriety and the financial rewards are great for those who make it, so here are a few basic hints.

There are several ways to go about getting a record deal, but it helps if you have someone behind you who will benefit from it too. A strong manager, publisher, or producer with contacts in the record business is much more likely to be able to get something together than you can do for yourself. They know the right people, have some leverage in the right places, and speak the language. Unless you are very unusual, you won't have the experience to wheel and deal a good recording contract for yourself. If you don't have anyone to speak for you, and you have to go directly to the company yourself, you can do one of several things:

1. Do A 'Live' Performance.

If you are performing in an area where there might be talent scouts for record companies (especially the larger cities with important clubs), invite a representative from the record company to hear you. It's best to find out the name of the person in charge of signing new talent, and send him a personal invitation followed by a phone call. Reserve a table and complimentary tickets and hope for the best. Many will simply not show up, but you might be surprised to find that one or two may actually come. Try to meet the person, let him know who you are and what you're into, and generally establish a rapport so he knows the kind of person he's dealing with. Do as tight and professional a show as you can, and play for maximum audience response, which is always very impressive.

2. Send A Tape.

Try to produce as professional a tape as you can. This may mean laying out some bread for a small studio, or commandeering some equipment from a friend who knows his way around a tape recorder and microphones, but do it right. Leave as little to the imagination as possible. Try to get the best musicians around, and the cleanest sound, highlighting your singing, playing, and songs. However, don't overproduce your tape or you may drown out what you are trying to sell. If you can't do it right with other musicians, then record your songs yourself in a straightforward, simple manner, playing and singing your very best material. Pick only three or four of your songs that show off contrasting aspects of your talent—any more and they won't be listened to. Program the material for maximum impact. Remember, the person listening is probably very busy, and he hears a dozen tapes a day, so you've got to impress him from the start.

Don't send in your only copy of the tape, because you probably won't get it back. Send tapes out to as many companies as you can, following them up with a phone call to try to get some answer and possibly an evaluation. If the person listening hears something he likes he may give you some constructive criticism to get you on the right track.

3. Do A 'Live' Audition.

This is the most difficult way to do it, both for you and for the record company representative who has to audition you. It may really pay off, though, if you are really together and can put yourself and your songs across in a straightforward, competent manner. The in-person audition will enable you to talk about your work, play some of your songs, and develop a personal relationship with the A&R man or recording executive you are meeting.

If the record company rejects you (*everyone* has been rejected at some time in his career) you are no worse off than you were before. If, by some chance, they show some interest in you, it's time to get a good lawyer. Recording contracts are long, involved, and devious, and it takes a practiced and knowledgeable mind to sort one out. Don't *ever* sign anything without a lawyer representing you whom you know has nothing but your interest at stake.

This brings us to another advantage of the small independent labels. The contracts are usually straightforward, simple, non-exclusive, and for only one album at a time. Since they don't have the power that money brings to the large corporations, the small labels can't tie you up for a long-term agreement; after you make your record you are free to try again where you please. Of course, the small company will hope that you'll show good faith and gratitude by continuing to record for them if your first record is a success, but that is entirely up to you.

The major disadvantage of recording for a small company is *distribution*, the key word in getting your *product* into the stores. Small, independent labels can put out the best music with the best intentions in the world, but as in films and books, the distribution is sewed up by the majors. Until very recently, the smaller companies, especially those dealing with "ethnic" folk music, could only be found in specialty shops, such as folklore centers, coffee houses, and in special bins of the large chain stores such as Sam Goody. Lately, inroads have been made because of the increasing demand for this kind of music. There has also been a large mail-order distribution setup that has been increasingly successful, so that albums may become more and more accessible, even though they have bypassed the distributors entirely.

The following list of folk-oriented independent labels is by no means complete, but it includes the most active and noteworthy of these labels.

Folkways Records (43 W. 61st St., New York, NY 10023). The oldest and largest company of its kind, documents the music, song, dance, and poetry of the world's peoples.

Rounder Records (186 Willow Ave., Somerville, MA 02144). Quickly becoming the most important producer of folk, bluegrass, and old-time music (including that of some younger musicians). Rounder also has one of the most comprehensive mail-order catalogs of hard-to-find labels.

Arhoolie (Box 9195, Berkeley, CA 94719). Mostly blues and funk, but occasionally Arhoolie records a "revival" folksinger. A terrific catalog of great blues guitarists.

Philo Records (Ferrisburg, VT 05473). Just a couple of years old, this Vermont company has its own 16-track studio and records young singer/songwriters. The statement on their albums declares that they "encourage the artists to assume full creative control of their albums. This record is as conceived of by the artist." What more could you ask?

Folk-Legacy (Sharon, CT 06069). Some traditional, some "revival" singers, mostly in the white ballad tradition. Many good solo singers.

Biograph Records (Box 109, Canaan, NY 12029). Although known originally for its re-issues of early country music, Biograph has been recording folk singers and bluegrass groups as well.

Kicking Mule Records (Box 3233, Berkeley, CA 94703). Founded by Stefan Grossman and ED Denson, this company is devoted to recording excellent guitar pickers for the benefit of the learning student. Motto: "Where the guitar is king."

Takoma (Box 5369, Santa Monica, CA 90405). This is John Fahey's company, and naturally it, too, emphasizes guitar playing, especially the free-form but folk-inspired fingerpicking of Fahey, Leo Kottke, Robbie Basho, and others.

There are dozens of other companies recording folk, country, and bluegrass artists. Look for ads and reviews in magazines such as *Pickin'*, *Guitar Player*, *Sing Out!*, *Muleskinner News*, etc. For larger companies' addresses, there is always *Rolling Stone*, *Billboard* (see their annual buyers' guide), *Cashbox*, and *Record World*. These trade magazines also carry some news of the activities of certain smaller labels, but their main emphasis is on the big guys.

THE UNIONS

At some point in your career you'll have to join a union, most likely The American Federation of Musicians. As long as you are playing local coffee houses or small college concerts it won't be necessary, but as soon as you start getting into the larger night clubs and doing recordings you'll have to join up.

The union's stated primary concern is to see that its members get a minimum wage, good working conditions, and decent hours to minimize the exploitation of working musicians by club owners, theater managers, promoters, or even other musicians. The unions set the "scale" or minimum wage (try to see that no member works for less than scale), enforce contracts, and in some cases provide pension plans, hospitalization, death benefits, insurance and other benefits —depending on the size and wealth of the particular local.

In return for these services, you pay an

initiation fee ($50 to $500, again depending on the local), annual dues, and a tax on each job you play in the local's jurisdiction. When you play out of town, you pay a "traveling tax" to the local in that area. It's a little like protection money; you kick a little into the union, and they protect you from the "bad guys" and make sure (or at least tell you they do) you get what's in the contract.

Once you are in the union you must file union contracts on all your gigs, play only with union members in good standing, appear only in union-authorized places, accept only union scale or better, and otherwise conform to the regulations set down in the local and national bylaws.

These rules and regulations can sometimes be a hassle, but I have found that as a folk singer/guitarist I have rarely encountered any problems in fulfilling union requirements. The unions were set up primarily to aid the more business-like situation of orchestra, dance band, and studio musicians who work regular jobs in which their relationship to their leader or employer is that of labor to management.

It seems to me that the union has never showed a great amount of interest in the more freewheeling folk or rock acts that do not fit the standard leader-sideman-employer format, and although folk and rock acts undoubtedly are benefited by the union, they need only have active contact with their local if they want to. I have been a union member for about twelve years, and I have only been asked to show my card at one club, and to my knowledge no union rep has ever checked out the working conditions of any of the various clubs or halls I have played, some of which were exceedingly seedy. Even so, I feel that it is important to belong to the union, both for the principle behind the union idea as well as for the small amount of protection they may give you in case you are ripped off.

Fortunately, the musicians' union is one of the few in the performing arts in which there are no apprenticeship requirements, patronage, exorbitant fees, or other impediments to joining. So when you are ready, you can contact your local and find out about getting an application.

JOAN BAEZ

FOLK GUITAR IN THE STUDIO

MARCEL DADI

A skilled, technically adept player can sometimes get involved in recording studio work and find financial and sometimes artistic rewards. Although the major folk recording work was done during the Sixties, it is still possible to get occasional work backing up folk singers who have a more basic guitar style. This type of accompaniment often requires equal portions of taste, steadiness, and flash, so it is essential to listen hard and long to backup guitarists on records until you get the feel for where the licks come in and how to develop the sensitivity that shows you how not to step on the singer's musical toes.

Many of the younger, folk-oriented singer/songwriters seem to be using electric guitarists to back up their acoustic strumming. The electric guitar gives their music a more modern, country-rock sound than the traditional acoustic-folk lead guitar playing. Although the emphasis of this book is on acoustic playing, you probably should be prepared for some electric work. There are some fine guitarists recording folk-style guitar though, including Dave Bromberg and Ry Cooder.

Being a studio sideman is a very specialized field, so I thought I'd find out some of the specifics of this kind of work from someone who does it all the time. I contacted an old friend, Eric Weissberg, and asked him some questions about the studio scene and how it works for him.

Eric has long been one of the most sought-after studio musicians who play in the folk style. Best known for his banjo work ("Dueling Banjos"), he is also accomplished on electric and acoustic guitar, pedal steel, mandolin, fiddle, and bass. After graduating from the High School of Music and Art, in New York, where he was the first student ever accepted on the merits of his banjo picking, Eric went on to study classical bass at the Juilliard School of Music and the University of Wisconsin. Throughout those years of academic work, Eric continued exploring every folk instrument he could get his hands on, recording solo albums of his 5-string banjo for small, folk-oriented labels. Before he settled into full-time studio work, he performed with the Tarriers, toured with Judy Collins, and recorded on dozens of albums as a backup musician.

H.T. Can you give us some idea of how you started out as a studio musician?
E.W. For me, getting into the steady studio thing was relatively easy, because in the early Sixties, just after I joined the Tarriers, folk music was at its hottest. Lots of people were recording in New York, and there was virtually nobody who could read music and play 5-string banjo, folk-style guitar,

mandolin, and fiddle. These were considered "weird" instruments that nobody played in the studios. So I broke in that way, playing mostly banjo on records and jingles (commercials). After a while I had to tell a few people I played more than just banjo. Every time I got called for a banjo date I would tell whoever ran the session that I play guitars and other instruments. Then I began to get called on the other stuff, too. It was a struggle at first, especially after I started doing only studio work when I left Judy Collins in 1966. I only made about $3,000 for the year, which is not a lot. But before that I was on the road with the Tarriers and whenever we were not on the road I'd do whatever I'd get called for. After the Tarriers broke up, I went with Judy for a year, then I came back and said I've gotta stop traveling and start doing what I really want to do, which is studio work—I happen to like it. So the first year was $3,000 and every subsequent year it just about doubled—partly from getting more dates and partly because scale went up.
H.T. Do you think you would have gotten all those jobs if you hadn't been able to read?
E.W. Well, the studio guitar players just didn't play folk styles. They played chunka-chunka or jazz chord-melody stuff—which I can't do at all—so in a way there was never competition, which was nice. I would have gotten calls even if I hadn't been able to read, but I think it made it easier for a producer because I could read; especially for jingles when you only have an hour to do the jingle and they want to get it finished. Not so much being able to read actual notes, which I still have trouble with on the guitar oddly enough; but it was being able to follow a conductor and being able to read at least the measures and where to play and where to lay out that helped.
H.T. When they give you a chart, is it actually written music or is it just chords and rhythms?
E.W. In those days, a lot of guys were trying to write out the notes of, say, a Merle Travis-type thing. I mean, really! They'd expect you to play it. But a lot of it was being able to

follow a conductor and a rhythm chart without struggling. A lot of times, if I got real complicated notes written out, I'd say to the guy, "Do you want me to play exactly what you've got here, or something in the style and feel that you want?" They'd always say "Play what's right," unless the guy was totally crazy, and I got into a couple of *insane* fights with guys—but that was very rare. Now, almost *nobody* writes notes for guitar, no matter what the style is. They give you a chord sheet, and sometimes the melody is there, but they'll say, "This is in this particular style, see what you can do with it."

H.T. Do New York studio musicians use the number system that Nashville musicians use?

E.W. No, but for me, that's easy because my theory training at Music and Art was numbers, so I'd have no trouble doing what they do in Nashville.

H.T. Do producers know anything about folk styles; will they say "play something in a Travis style, or a Doc Watson style?"

E.W. Most of them aren't that hip. There are some, like Walter Raim, who knows exactly what's happening. Walter is doing a lot of writing now, and a lot of his stuff is in picking styles. Oddly enough, he is one of the few people who writes out a lot of stuff. So I know now to get there twenty minutes early and he'll be there and he'll sit down with the guitar and show me what it's supposed to sound like. He plays that style, so he knows how to write it.

H.T. Now you're talking about jingles, where you've got to go in and just knock them out. What about folk albums? I know you've played on a lot of those.

E.W. Well, I did a lot of playing for the Brothers Four, Judy Collins, and John Denver. I can't even think of too many others right now.

H.T. Did you get charts for those sessions, or did you just work the tunes out with the artists?

E.W. It would depend on the producer. The Brothers Four were produced by Teo Macero. Milt Okun, who was their musical director, used to write everything out. They worked out their arrangements with him, and he would write a chart out. But it was easy as pie, since the chords were simple, and if he said "play chunka-chunka" or "do some picking," I'd play it. They never bugged me about anything. I've been working with Judy on her new album, and she's got a new producer who is writing chord charts out. But still, it's very loose. We'll get in there and he'll take out a measure here or there if it doesn't feel right, and everybody in the band seems to be contributing. And the charts are there so you have something in front of you for you to say, "Look, we're taking out Bar 36," because half the band doesn't know the song and they're really just reading it.

H.T. Do you find that the younger musicians who are playing guitar or related instruments are familiar with folk styles and have a background in folk music?

E.W. No, I think most of the guys in my generation—between 25 and 35—who are playing guitar now are much more rock and blues oriented. But by now there's so much folk-type music that's popular—with Judy and James Taylor, Carly Simon, and so on—that you have to know what the folk styles feel like. The studio musicians can create that feel, although many times nowadays you don't *want* only that feel. For instance, we did "City Of New Orleans" with Judy Collins, which is really a folk song, but Hugh McCracken played these little blues licks in there, and it sounds fantastic. The combination is sometimes great. It makes it exciting. Otherwise it's just formula stuff (which is what the Brothers Four did).

H.T. What do you think someone would have to do to break into the studio field? It seems like a really closed circuit.

E.W. It is closed, but I see new guys all the time. Each year there's two or three new guitar players on the scene.

H.T. Is it an all-around ability in different areas that is wanted, or do people still specialize? For instance, if the producer wanted a folk-type date, would he call certain people? And if they wanted a jazz-type date they wouldn't call the folk people, but would call someone who is a good jazz player?

E.W. It works both ways. You have to be good to break in, there's no getting around that. You can't go in there and fake it. Everyone will know immediately. Versatility really does help. First of all, there really aren't that many dates around. If I do twelve dates a week, that's a lot. There are all different kinds of dates. If I just specialized in folk, one date a week would be a lot. So, you have to be versatile, and you have to get a lucky break. Maybe you're playing with a band and the leader of the band gets called so he brings you with him. And there's a few steady studio guys on the date who hear you and like the way you play, so they write your name in their book and it builds up that way.

H.T. Let's say there's a player reading this book somewhere. He's been practicing his butt off for six years and really thinks he has it together. But he's never really been anywhere and doesn't know anybody. What can he do?

E.W. Well, it's the first one that's really the hardest. You can't just hang around a studio and wait for somebody to show up. I'm sure it's been done but I wouldn't recommend it.

H.T. I take it there aren't as many gigs for backing up folk groups in the studios as there used to be in the Sixties.

E.W. A lot of those people have drifted off into different scenes. I can't even think of who's doing what kind of thing now.

H.T. What's scale now?

E.W. $100 per session.

H.T. What happens when you get in the studio with the pedal steel; do you read music for that?

E.W. Number one: Nobody knows how to write for pedal steel, so they may write the melody of the tune out, but they never write specifically for the instrument. The steel is one instrument where you can't be reading and playing at the same time, because you have to look at the fingerboard. There are no frets, so a lot of it is trying to memorize real quick, which can be a drag on the jingle date. I actually do a lot of steel dates, because there is nobody else who plays and is around a lot. Bill Keith is on the road a lot, and Winnie Winston is in

Philadelphia. So if they want a steel sound on a date, they've got to call me. If I didn't play a lot of these odd-ball instruments, I'd be selling shoes or something. I mean, there's still virtually no one in the New York studio scene who plays 5-string. Dick Weissman moved to Colorado. I recommend Barry Kornfeld, Steve Mandell, and that's about it. There have been a lot of steel dates, and since "Dueling Banjos" I've been getting a lot more banjo dates again. I also get some fiddle, mandolin, and Dobro work, but still there's a lot of guitar. I do about 300 dates a year now, and about 50% on guitar and the other 50% divided among the other instruments.

H.T. Is it primarily acoustic or electric guitar that you get called for?

E.W. I haven't figured that out. A lot of times they'll ask you to bring both, since they don't know what sound they want until they get in the studio. I play a lot of rhythm guitar, and sometimes I play fills or lead parts, depending on what the music is and if there's another guitar player. I'm not going to do any lead work if Hugh McCracken or Charlie Brown or Dave Spinoza is there. I don't consider myself a really great lead rock player, by any stretch of the imagination. I can do it on a jingle if they just want a certain feel. Otherwise, I like playing rhythm. I enjoy it. I also like to listen to these guys, who are so good, doing what they do best on guitar.

H.T. Do you think there's something besides ability that gets you so many studio calls?

E.W. I'm very reliable, hardly ever late which is very important in session work. I'm also a reliable player, not super-flashy or anything but I have good time, and I always get the feel that they want—especially on the rhythm stuff. Most of the guys have known me for a long time and they know all of that. Plus, I think some still comes from "Dueling Banjos."

H.T. Who calls you for a date?

E.W. It can be any number of people. The union regulation says there has to be a contractor if there's more than eight players on a date, so if it's a big date the contractor will call you. A lot of times it's the arranger or the producer or even a representative of the company. One interesting sidelight of playing unusual instruments like pedal steel and banjo is that sometimes they'll book me at my convenience and then get the rest of the band together around that, because they want the particular sound I can furnish before they call the other instruments that are easier to get players for.

H.T. Do you remember your first record date as a session man?

E.W. I remember an early one, maybe not *the* first, but it's very vivid in my mind. It was a big date at what is now A&M, but it was Columbia then. In those days I used to get to a date early and look over the guitar parts and pick out the easiest one, with the least amount of notes. Well, I got to this date and there were three or four guitar chairs, with the music already out. I look at the music and on the music sheet itself it says "Guitar 1 —Eric." I said, "Holy crap!" Then the guys began to dribble in and it was like the top guys—I mean, Al Caiola! I really began to sweat. I had never seen anybody's name on the music before—in fact, I think mine was the only name on there. So these guys came in and introduced themselves and I was embarrassed—Guitar 1—me! But it was terrific, because they sat down and couldn't have cared less which part they played, and it all went okay.

AFTERWORD

MANCE LIPSCOMB

In reseaching this book, I was more than ever made aware of the dichotomy between the commercially oriented, corporate, big star/big money approach to music (specifically folk music), and the more grassroots, traditional, personalized music that most people associate with the term "folk." The representatives of the former philosophy (if you will), the agents, publishers, record company executives, etc. were on the whole pessimistic and discouraging, speaking of the vagaries of the market, tight money, slower record sales and the concomitant cutting back of artist rosters, and putting forth the demise of the "folksinger" as a reality of the marketplace. On the other hand, the "folkies," representing a more freewheeling, disassociated, alternative lifestyle approach, while not having anywhere near the money or the mass appeal of the commercial music makers, were, on the whole, optimistic and fully enjoying the *process* of music making and communicating with their fellows on many different levels. Folk and bluegrass magazines such as *Sing Out!* and *Pickin'* are experiencing an unprecedented rise in popularity, and mainstream publications such as *Rolling Stone* and *Guitar Player* are consistently devoting a good proportion of their space to folk, country, and bluegrass music. Small festivals are thriving all over the country and are growing in number each year, and record companies such as Rounder, Folkways, Arhoolie, Kicking Mule, and Yazoo are staying alive through an almost underground approach to sales and customers. This is not to say that many folk-style performers and singer/songwriters are not embittered and discouraged by the lack of interest by the mass media, or by their relative poverty in a marketplace of hundreds of millions of dollars disproportionately fed into the vaults of larger and larger corporations. Fame, money, acceptance, ego-gratification are all part of the rewards of being a successful artist, but in many cases the gratification that the folk artists are seeking is more in terms of the deeper and more long-lasting values that go with really communicating with the public.

The distinctions between the two ends of the pop-folk spectrum are somewhat blurred by the success of certain folk-oriented groups on the rock circuit and, conversely, the necessity of some pop stars to fall back on the folk festival/coffee house circuit to maintain their following and identity. I should add that I am not trying to make a purist judgment of one approach over the other, although I'm sure my preference is obvious. What is important to me is that this book gives as clear a picture as possible of the various ways that one can make it as a "professional folk guitarist," and, although each person will give or receive an answer according to his own view of the situation, the rewards are there for the taking. You will succeed through talent, perseverance, knowledge, friends, fortitude, and all the other traits that make a person a winner. The path you choose will ultimately be as a result of trial and error, and as you make your way through the labyrinth, enjoy the puzzle as much as the solution. What you do with yourself at the other end will be entirely up to you.

APPENDIX

HAPPY TRAUM / BOX 694, WOODSTOCK, NEW YORK 12498

PUBLICITY PICTURE

Happy Traum

FOLK GUITARIST

For booking information, contact Homespun Music
Box 694, Woodstock, NY 12498 800-555-1212

SAMPLE BUSINESS CARD

Happy Traum

SAMPLE BROCHURE CONTENTS

Records by Happy Traum

Broadside (Folkways) - with Bob Dylan (Blind Boy Grunt), Phil Ochs, Pete Seeger, and others.

The New World Singers (Atlantic) - "Listen to the New World Singers. . .they sing like they know who they are." - Bob Dylan

Happy and Artie Traum (Capitol) - "One of the best records in any field of pop music" - New York Times

Double Back (Capitol) - "They create songs which are musically tight and lyrically intelligent. . . .This is a record that can mean something to you personally." - Crawdaddy

Mud Acres (Rounder) - "It might have been the best record of 1972" - City Magazine

---

"Happy Traum was marvelous! He was beautiful, warm and giving, as always." *

Happy Traum's performances reflect his vast experience in the world of folk, blues, and country music. His versatility as a singer, instrumentalist, and songwriter have brought him critical acclaim across the U.S., England and Europe.

Although best known for his appearances and recordings with his brother Artie and their band, he has toured widely as a solo performer and as a member of several folk and rock groups. As an instrumentalist, he has recorded and performed with Bob Dylan, Maria Muldaur, Allen Ginsberg, Jean Ritchie, and many others.

In addition to his live and recorded performances, Happy Traum is the author of over a dozen best-selling guitar instruction books, and is a frequent contributor to Rolling Stone, Crawdaddy, Sing Out!, Guitar Player, and other magazines. Writing about Happy and Artie, The New York Times has said:

"Between them they've been studio musicians, composers, comedians, writers, editors, folklorists, and a host of other things. . . .A brilliant and unique entity in the world of country-folk music."

An evening with Happy Traum might include guitar and banjo instrumentals, traditional and contemporary ballads, Delta blues, and even a song or two in which the audience feels moved to add their voices to his. Whatever he pulls out of his songbag, Happy has a unique knack for making his listeners feel at home, turning the largest hall into an intimate room.

* Woodstock Times review of Happy Traum/Allen Ginsberg concert, Dec. 1974.

**For booking information, contact
Jane Traum, Homespun Music, Box 694,
Woodstock, NY 12498   (914) 551-1212**

BIO/RESUME

Happy Traum has been an active and important figure on the music scene for more than fifteen years. His avid interest in folk, blues, country, and old-time music have brought him recognition in many musical areas: as a teacher, writer, recording artist, editor, folk-lorist, and performer.

Born on May 9, 1938, Happy began playing guitar and 5-string banjo while a student at New York's High School of Music and Art. In 1957-'58 he studied blues guitar with Brownie McGhee (with whom he later toured and co-authored a book), during which time he began singing and playing professionally. A full-time musician since 1960, Happy has recorded and toured extensively throughout the U.S. and Canada, both as a soloist and as a member of several folk and rock groups. Aside from his solo work, he is probably best known for his performan-ces, both live and recorded, with his brother, Artie.

The following is a partial listing of his appearances and publications:

CLUBS

The Bottom Line, Gerde's Folk City, The Bitter End, Max's Kansas City, The Metro Club (New York City); The Main Point (Philadelphia); Childe Harold (Washington, D.C.); Troubador (Los Angeles); The Boarding House (San Francisco); The Gate of Horn (Chicago); Potpourri (Mont-real); The Riverboat (Toronto).

CONCERTS

Carnegie Hall, Town Hall, Folklore Center (New York City); Woodstock Playhouse (Woodstock, N.Y.); Long Wharf Theater (New Haven, Conn.) Palace Theater (Albany, N.Y.); Colleges and Universities throughout the U.S.

FESTIVALS

Newport Folk Festival; Philadelphia Folk Festival; Fox Hollow Festival; Festival of American Folklife (Washington, D.C.); Culpepper Bluegrass Festival (Virginia); Winfield (Kansas) Blue-grass Festival; Folklife Festival - Expo '70 (Montreal, Canada); Cambridge (England) Folk Festival; Festival Pop Celtique (Brittany, France); Bilzen (Belgium) Jazz Festival.

RECORDINGS

Broadside - Vol.1 (Folkways) with Pete Seeger, Bob Dylan, Phil Ochs, etc.

The New World Singers (Atlantic)

Happy and Artie Traum (Capitol)

Double Back (Capitol)

Mud Acres (Rounder) with Maria Muldaur, John Herald, Bill Keith, etc.

Hard Times In The Country (Rounder)

Relax Your Mind (Kicking Mule - to be released January, 1976)

Happy Traum also appears as a back-up musician on record by Bob Dylan, Jean Ritchie, Chris Smither, Allen Ginsberg, and others.

BOOKS

Fingerpicking Styles for Guitar; Traditional and Contemporary Finger-picking; Guitar Styles of Brownie McGhee; Flatpick Country Guitar; Bluegrass Guitar (Oak Publications); The Blues Bag; Rock Guitar; The Children's Guitar Guide; The Young Guitarist; The Guitarist's Chord Manual; The Joy of the Guitar.

Editor of: The James Taylor Songbook; Arlo Guthrie; Incredible String Band; Eric Andersen; Pat Sky; Hard Hitting Songs for Hard Hit People.

Magazine contributions: Sing Out! (Editor, 1968-1971); Guitar Player (monthly column "Strictly Folk" since 1970); occasional articles and reviews have appeared in Rolling Stone, Crawdaddy, and other periodicals.

Happy Traum is also the founder of Homespun Tapes, which provides musical instruction on tapes and cassettes in guitar and banjo styles and blues piano by professional musicians. They have thousands of students all over the world.

AMERICAN FOLK AGENCY

1202 EAST SUNSET BOULEVARD, HOLLYWOOD, CA 90401   PHONE (213) 555-1212

THIS CONTRACT for the personal services of musicians on the engagement described below, made this_____day of
_____19____, between the undersigned Purchaser of Music (herein called "Employer") and_____musicians.
(including leader)

The musicians are engaged severally on the terms and conditions on the face hereof. The leader represents that the musicians already designated have agreed to be bound by said terms and conditions. Each musician yet to be chosen, upon acceptance, shall be bound by said terms and conditions. Each musician may enforce this agreement. The musicians severally agree to render services under the undersigned leader.

1. Name and Address of Place of Engagement_____

   Print Name of Band or Group_____

2. Date(s), starting and finishing time of engagement_____

   _____

3. Type of Engagement (specify whether dance, stage show, banquet, etc.)_____

   _____

4. WAGE AGREED UPON $_____
   (Terms and Amount)

   This wage includes expenses agreed to be reimbursed by the employer in accordance with the attached schedule or a schedule to be furnished the Employer on or before the date of engagement.

5. Employer will make payments as follows: _____
   (Specify when payments are to be made)

_____

Upon request by the Federation or the local in whose jurisdiction the musicians shall perform hereunder, Employer either shall make advance payment hereunder or shall post an appropriate bond.

If the engagement is subject to contribution to the A.F.M. & E.P.W. Pension Welfare Fund, the leader will collect same from the Employer and pay it to the Fund; and the Employer and leader agree to be bound by the Trust Indenture dated October 2, 1959, as amended, relating to services rendered hereunder in the U. S., and by the Agreement and Declaration of Trust dated April 9, 1962, as amended, relating to services rendered hereunder in Canada.

6. The Employer shall at all times have complete supervision, direction and control over the services of musicians on this engagement and expressly reserves the right to control the manner, means and details of the performance of services by the musicians including the leader as well as the ends to be accomplished. If any musicians have not been chosen upon the signing of this contract, the leader shall, as agent for the Employer and under his instructions, hire such persons and any replacements as are required.

7. The Employer hereby acknowledges his liability to provide workmen's compensation insurance and to pay social security and unemployment insurance taxes if same are applicable to the services to be rendered hereunder.

8. In accordance with the Constitution, By-laws, Rules and Regulations of the Federation, the parties will submit every claim, dispute, controversy or difference involving the musical services arising out of or connected with this contract and the engagement covered thereby for determination by the International Executive Board of the Federation or a similar board of an appropriate local thereof and such determination shall be conclusive, final and binding upon the parties.

Additional Terms and Conditions

The leader shall, as agent of the Employer, enforce disciplinary measures for just cause, and carry out instructions as to selections and manner of performance. The agreement of the musicians to perform is subject to proven detention by sickness, accidents, riots, strikes, epidemics, acts of God, or any other legitimate conditions beyond their control. On behalf of the Employer the leader will distribute the amount received from the Employer to the musicians, including himself as indicated on the opposite side of this contract, or in place thereof on separate memorandum supplied to the Employer at or before the commencement of the employment hereunder and take and turn over to the Employer receipts therefor from each musician, including himself. The amount paid to the leader includes the cost of transportation, which will be reported by the leader to the Employer.

All employees covered by this agreement must be members in good standing of the Federation. However, if the employment provided for hereunder is subject to the Labor-Management Relations Act, 1947, all employees who are members of the Federation when their employment commences hereunder shall be continued in such employment only so long as they continue such membership in good standing. All other employees covered by this agreement, on or before the thirtieth day following the commencement of their employment, or the effective date of this agreement, whichever is later, shall become and continue to be members in good standing of the Federation. The provisions of this paragraph shall not become effective unless and until permitted by applicable law.

To the extent permitted by applicable law, nothing in this contract shall ever be construed so as to interfere with any duty owing by any musician performing hereunder to the Federation pursuant to its Constitution, By-laws, Rules, Regulations and Orders. *(Continued on reverse side)*

X_____ X_____
Print Employer's Name   Print Leader's Name   Local No.

_____   _____
Signature of Employer   Signature of Leader

_____   _____
Print Street Address   Leader's Home Address

City	State	Zip Code	City	State	Zip Code
					3854

Telephone   Booking Agent   Agreement No.

*Standard union contract form.   LEADER'S COPY   FORM B-3B   REV. 7-70   44

Additional Terms and Conditions (continued)

Any musicians on this engagement are free to cease service hereunder by reason of any strike, ban, unfair list order or requirement of the Federation or of any Federation local approved by the Federation or by reason of any other labor dispute approved by the Federation, and shall be free to accept and engage in other employment of the same or similar character or otherwise, without any restraint, hindrance, penalty, obligation or liability whatever, any other provisions of this contract to the contrary notwithstanding.

Representatives of the Federation local in whose jurisdiction the musicians shall perform hereunder shall have access to the place of performance (except to private residences) for the purpose of conferring with the musicians.

No performance on the engagement shall be recorded, reproduced or transmitted from the place of performance, in any manner or by any means whatsoever, in the absence of a specific written agreement with the Federation relating to and permitting such recording, reproduction or transmission.

The Employer represents that there does not exist against him, in favor of any member of the Federation, any claim of any kind arising out of musical services rendered for such Employer. No musician will be required to perform any provisions of this contract or to render any services for said Employer as long as any such claim is unsatisfied or unpaid, in whole or in part. If the Employer breaches this agreement, he shall pay the musicians in addition to damages, 6% interest thereon plus a reasonable attorney's fee.

To the extent permitted by applicable law, all of the Constitution, By-laws, Rules and Regulations of the Federation and of any local thereof applicable to this engagement (not in conflict with those of the Federation) will be adhered to and the parties acknowledge that they are and each has the obligation to be, fully acquainted therewith.

10-70

Names of Musicians	A.F.M. Local and U.S. Social Security Numbers (if any)		Direct Pay; and Pension Fund Contributions (where applicable)	
			$	$
_____ Leader				

AMERICAN FOLK AGENCY

1202 EAST SUNSET BOULEVARD, HOLLYWOOD, CA 90401   PHONE (213) 555-1212

RIDER to agreement dated _____January 24, 1972_____ between

_____Happy and Artie Traum_____ Artist ("Corporation")

and ___Gaslight II_____ Employer.

1. The following provisions shall be deemed incorporated in and part of the agreement to which this Rider is annexed:

2. All payments by the Employer to Corporation required to be made under or pursuant to this agreement, shall be made in the form of cash, money order, certified check, cashier's check, or in the case of concerts performed and for a University, by a check drawn on a University account. Payment by cashier's check or certified check is requested. Artist may refuse to accept a personal check as fulfillment of any portion of Employer's obligation hereunder. If any balance remains to be paid on the fee hereunder at the time the performance commences, such balance shall be paid to Artist's representative prior to or immediately upon commencement of Artist's performance. In the event that the compensation payable to Corporation hereunder is measured in whole or in part by a percentage of receipts, Employer shall pay Artist's representative the balance of the guaranteed amount PRIOR to Artist's performance, in one of the forms specified above. Any balance subsequently due on a percentage computation will be paid as soon as practicable after the closing of the box office, and unless extreme circumstances make it impossible, this will be no later than one half-hour before the end of Artist's last performance hereunder. At that time a ticket printer's manifest and a detailed box office statement will be given to Artist's representative.

3. All gross admission receipts shall be computed on the actual full admission price provided on each ticket, and, in the absence of prior written agreement by Artist, no ticket shall be offered or sold at a discount or a premium. All tickets shall be serially numbered and sold consecutively.

4. All payments shall be made as provided herein. In the event employer fails to make any payment at the time stipulated herein or breaches any other provision of this agreement, Artist shall have the right to withhold performance without prejudice to his rights hereunder.

5. Employer warrants that tickets for the engagement will be scaled in the following prices:

_____TICKETS at _____dollars each

_____TICKETS at _____dollars each

_____TICKETS at _____dollars each

If the scale of prices shall be varied in any respect, the percentage compensation payable to Artist shall be based upon whichever of the following is more favorable to the Artist: the scale of prices as set forth above, or the actual scale of prices in effect for the engagement.

6. In the event that compensation payable to Corporation hereunder is measured in whole or in part by a percentage of receipts, Corporation shall have the right to set a limit to the number of free admissions authorized by Employer. If the Employer is unable to accurately determine the number of persons admitted free, the Employer agrees to accept as binding a reasonable estimate made by the Artist's road manager.

7. A representative of the Artist shall have the right to be present in the box office prior to and during the performance and intermission periods and such representative shall be given full access to all box office sales and shall otherwise be permitted to reasonably satisfy himself as to the gross receipts (and expenditures if required) at each performance hereunder.

8. Employer agrees to have on hand at the place of performance on the night of the show for counting verification by a representative of Artist or the Agency all unsold tickets. Artist shall be compensated for all seats as shown by manifest for which there is not an unsold ticket on hand, minus approved complimentary tickets. Unless an unsold ticket is shown to Artist's representative, it shall be deemed that employer has sold a ticket for that seat at the highest price that seat could have sold for.

9. Any promotional material which Employer may use, including posters, flyers, or handbills, or publicity containing the Artist's name, likeness, caricature or biographies shall be so used only for the purposes of promoting the concert. In no event may any such materials be sold or marketed in any manner by Employer.

10. In the event Employer shall breach this agreement, Artist shall have the right without limiting any of its other remedies hereunder to refrain from rendering a performance or to stop rendering a performance if such breach occurs during the rendition of a performance. Notwithstanding the cessation of such performance, Employer shall be liable to Artist for all of the fees and compensation hereunder in the same manner as though Artist had fully performed. A breach of any clause contained in this rider by the Employer shall be deemed a material breach. If Artist elects to perform or continue to perform notwithstanding a breach of this agreement by Employer, the performance by Artist shall not constitute a waiver of any claim the Artist may have for damages or otherwise.

11. Artist shall have sole and exclusive control over the production, presentation and performance of his portion of the engagement hereunder, and Artist shall have the sole right, as Artist shall see fit, to designate and change at any time his performing personnel. Artist's obligations hereunder are subject to detention or prevention by sickness, inability to perform, accident, means of transportation, act of God, riots, strikes, labor difficulties, epidemics, any act or order of public authority or any other cause, similar or dissimilar, beyond Artist's control.

12. If before the date of the engagement contracted for herein it is found that Employer has not fully performed his obligations under any other agreement with Artist or with any other party or that the financial credit of the Employer has been seriously impaired, Artist may require that Employer immediately pay in full all guaranteed amounts, regardless of the fact that a deposit had already been paid, or that a deposit was waived. If Employer fails for any reason to make such payment in full within 48 hours after such written request has been made by Artist, then such failure shall be considered an anticipatory breach of the entire contract and Artist may immediately sue for the balance of the contract fee. In the event Employer does not perform all of his obligations hereunder, Artist shall have the option to perform or refuse to perform hereunder and in either event Employer shall be liable to Artist for damages in addition to the compensation provided herein.

13. Employer shall provide a comfortable and private dressing room, adequate for use by 10 persons. This room shall be clean, dry, well-lit, heated or air-conditioned, shall contain at least 10 chairs and shall be within easy access to clean lavatories which are supplied with soap, toilet tissue and towels. These lavatories shall be closed to the general public. Employer shall be solely responsible for the security of items in the dressing area and shall keep all unauthorized persons from entering said area.

14. An ample supply of hot coffee, tea, soft drinks (no artificially sweetened drinks), beer, cold water, hot and cold cups with appropriate condiments (sugar, cream, lemon and honey) shall be provided in the dressing room at least two hours prior to the performance.

15. Artist shall receive 100% star billing in any and all publicity releases and paid advertisements, including without limitation, programs, flyers, signs, lobby boards, tickets and marquees. No other performer will receive credit or billing on the same publicity release or advertisement, etc. without prior written approval of Artist.

16. No other act may appear on the same program without the prior written approval of Artist.

17. Where two separate shows, i.e. playing for two separate audiences, are contemplated under the terms of this contract, Employer at his sole cost and expense will provide an opening act which must be approved of in writing at least two weeks before the date of the engagement hereunder by Artist.

18. The place of performance will be completely ready and available to Artist for a sound check at least five hours prior to performance.

19. Artist does not perform with audience seated on all sides of the stage, i.e. in the round. If such a performance is contemplated by Employer, Employer must first obtain the written permission of Artist through his agent.

20. Employer shall not allow the audience to enter the place of performance until such time as technical set-up has been completed. Artist shall complete said set-up one hour prior to time of performance provided that Employer makes

the place of performance available for said set-up at least five hours prior to the time of the performance.

21. Artist shall not be required to appear or perform before any audience which is segregated on the basis of race, color, creed or where physical violence or injury to Artist is likely to occur.

If any of the foregoing conditions exist and Artist does not appear or perform as a result thereof, the same shall not constitute a breach of this agreement by Artist.

22. NO PORTION OF THE PERFORMANCE RENDERED HEREUNDER MAY BE BROADCAST, PHOTO-GRAPHED, RECORDED, FILMED, TAPED OR EMBODIED IN ANY FORM FOR ANY PURPOSE OF REPRODUCING SUCH PERFORMANCE AND EMPLOYER AGREES THAT IT WILL NOT AUTHORIZE ANY SUCH RECORDING. EMPLOYER WILL DENY ENTRANCE TO ANY PERSONS CARRYING AUDIO OR VIDEO RECORDING DEVICES. WITHOUT LIMITING IN ANY WAY THE GENERALITY OF THE FOREGOING PROHIBITION, IT IS UNDERSTOOD TO INCLUDE MEMBERS OF THE AUDIENCE, PRESS AND EMPLOYER'S STAFF.

23. Artist shall have the exclusive right to sell or cause to be sold souvenir booklets or other publications of any kind or nature at or during the place of engagement. No product or publication utilizing the names and/or likenesses of Artist or one or more of them, may be produced, sold or distributed by any other person, firm or corporation without prior written consent of the Artist.

24. In the case of an open promotion, Employer shall commence public advertising at least three weeks prior to the date of the first performance.

25. Artist shall have the right to cancel this agreement without liability upon notice to Employer no later than forty-five days prior to the date of the first performance hereunder in the event Artist secures a commitment for a motion picture, a major television guest appearance, a series of television performances, a "Special" television program or a legitimate stage production, and such commitment would/might interfere or conflict with the engagement hereunder.

26. In the event of a breach of this agreement by Artist, Employer's damages shall be limited to necessary out-of-pocket expenses which were directly incurred for the performances covered by this contract. In no case shall such damage exceed $1,000.00.

27. It is specifically agreed and understood that a representative of Artist shall have sole and absolute authority in mixing and controlling all sound equipment while Artist is performing. (Where strict union requirements make this impossible, highly competent union personnel must be supplied and must take directions from Artist's representative).

28. In order to insure the punctual presentation of the performance contracted for hereunder and rapid correction of any problems which may occur, Artist's road manager, sound man, equipment men and musicians shall be supplied with whatever identification and authorization which may be necessary for complete freedom of movement throughout place of performance (theater, pavillion, stadium, ball park or other). These passes must be good for back stage, stage, dressing room, main

audience area and parking areas. These passes in order to be received by Artist
and Artist's service crew must be received at the Agency office no later than seven
days prior to the date of engagement.

29. This agreement may not be changed, modified or altered except by an instrument in writing, signed by the parties. This agreement shall be construed in
accordance with the laws of the State of New York. Any claim or dispute arising
out of or relating to this agreement or the breach thereof shall be settled
by arbitration in New York, New York in accordance with the rules and regulations
then obtained of the American Arbitration Association governing the three member
panels.

30. Any proposed additional terms and conditions which may be affixed to
this contract by Employer do not become part of this contract until signed
by Artist or by Artist's Management. By the sole act of signing Employer
fully accepts all provisions of Artist's contract regardless of any deletions
or additions he may attempt to make.

31. The Agency, as the corporate agent, of Artist assumes no personal liability
for any act or omission of Artist, or employees of Artist.

32. Employer shall furnish and provide the following at its sole cost and
expense:

    (a) A stage area 40' wide and 25' deep for the exclusive use of the
Artist. Employer agrees that this stage area will be kept free of
people and equipment during the time that it is assigned to Artist.
Employer further agrees that if the engagement is to be outdoors
there will be a covering over the stage that will protect Artist
and equipment from the elements to Artist's satisfaction. In the
event that it is necessary for the Employer to have other artists,
their employees and equipment on this stage during the time assigned
to Artist, Employer agrees that they will not occupy the space
allocated to Artist, and that their presence will be concealed from
the audience by means of curtains, drops or screens.

    (b) Adequate security personnel in uniform for the protection of Artist;
persons who travel with Artist and personal property of Artist and
said persons. Such security personnel will be available during
rehearsals (if necessary), performances, and for at least one-half
hour after performances. One guard for the dressing room is to
guard the dressing room during the entire time the room is in use.
The Artist's managers shall have sole control of placement of the
stage guards.

    (c) Adequate electrical service and electrical facilities to be installed
by licensed electricians and professional personnel in accordance
with the standards of the community.

    (d) All necessary permits, licenses and authorizations from any and all
government agencies, bureaus and departments, Federal, State or
local.

    (e) Any and all necessary immigration clearances if concert is to be
performed outside the U.S.A.

(f) Access to place of performance for unloading equipment.

(g) Parking space for two cars and one truck in close proximity and with direct access to stage door, for a period commencing five hours prior to performance and for two hours after.

(h) A maximum of 50 complimentary tickets located in preferred seating locations for use by the persons designated by Artist.

(i) Employer will provide, at its sole cost and expense, an adequate professional stage lighting system with a minimum of 2 spotlights and standard assortment of colored gels or any combination or variation thereof acceptable to Artist. Each color gel must be independently controllable. If Employer provides a "psychedelic" or other light show, Artist specifically reserves the right to request that such light show be turned off during the performance and Employer agrees to comply with such request at the time it is made.

(j) A four position head-set intercom system (head-set; telex 500 or similar) to be used for communication between Artist's sound man at sound mixing board, light board, and each follow-spot operator.

(k) An adequate public address system from one of the suppliers on the accompanying list. Employer agrees to cooperate fully with Corporation, Agency, and the specified P.A. suppliers in order to present Artist in a manner which does not compromise his standards of performance. If Employer feels it is able to supply adequate sound amplification with its own system, it must obtain prior written permission from Corporation or Agency before doing so. Any system supplied by Employer must, in every detail, meet or exceed the specifications as set forth in the attached rider for sound systems.

32. A representative of Artist shall have final approval of staging. Artist's sound man will give lighting cue by a radio-set intercom from the sound mixing board.

33. In the case of any conflict of terms, the terms contained herein shall prevail over any other including any printed, hand-written, or typed terms located elsewhere in this contract. All terms are specifically accepted by Employer unless they are waived by Artist or his representative. Such waiver shall be effective only if initialed by both Artist and Employer.

34. All payments hereunder shall be made payable to Art and Happy Traum.

35. The above constitutes the sole, complete and binding agreement between the parties hereto.

_____   _____
EMPLOYER   DATE

_____   _____
ART AND HAPPY TRAUM   DATE

ARTIE AND HAPPY TRAUM

TECHNICAL RIDER FOR SOUND SYSTEM

1.   Employer shall provide a vocal reinforcement system (public address
system) capable of delivering 115 DB S.P.L. of undistorted vocal sound
over a frequency range of at least 80 to 100 CPS, measured at 30 feet
from the stage with a decrease in level of no greater than 6 DB per 100
feet thereafter with no peaks or lobes in excess of 8 DB.

2.   This vocal reinforcement system shall have no fewer than 12 low impedence input channels to the mixer with adequate output facilities to
match the amplification.

3.   This vocal reinforcement system shall be driven by amplifiers having
a total combined output power of not less than 1,500 watts RMS.

4.   The speaker system shall have no less than the combined low frequency
radiating area of eight 15" low frequency loud speakers. The high fre-.
quency reproducers shall be of high efficiency horn and driver type with
a frequency response of 500 to 10,000 CPS and power handling of no less
than 100 watts per high frequency driver.

5.   The vocal reinforcement system shall be 12 low impedence microphones
of the following types or their qualitative equivalents:

                    Shure #565
                    SM-56, SMK-57, SM-58
                    Electrovoice - RE-10, RE-15, AKGD1, 000

All microphones must be equipped with pop filters or wind screens.

6.   The vocal reinforcement monitor system shall include at least one
monitor speaker per vocalist or no fewer than three speakers per group
of equal quality to the main speaker system. Speakers shall have special
volume control.

7.   No speaker system having loud speaker clusters more than 30 feet from
center stage shall be acceptable (ceiling-hung loud speaker clusters or
distributed systems.).

The listed sound contractors are proven leaders in their field and have
provided superb sound for numerous artists in the past. Should any
problem arise concerning sound, you may feel confident in consulting
the listed distributors.